'An enlightening read, a playbook for new international financial architecture of one of the leading European visionaries…'.

Frank Van Gansbeke, *Executive Scholar in Residence at Middlebury College (US) and co-founder Beyond Bretton Woods*

'This book is a wise and powerful critique of the current global financial system. It must be read now. Otherwise, a few decades later, we will wish to have read it but it will be too late then'.

Professor Vedat Akgiray, *Director of the Center for Research in Financial Regulation and Corporate Governance, Bogazici University, Turkey, Former Chairman for IOSCO Emerging Markets Committee, and Chairman of Capital Markets Authorities Forum under COMCEC, Vice Chairman of the IOSCO Board for the period of 2012–2014*

'Brunnhuber sets out a way, employing critically underused tools left over from the old, such as Special Drawing Rights and AAA-rated, not-for-profit development banks lending to poorly rated countries at the centre of the system'.

Avinash Persaud, *former architect of the Bridgetown Initiative 1.0 for international financial reform, a climate finance negotiator within the UNFCCC, currently special advisor on Climate Change to the President of the Inter-American Development Bank*

'Financing for development: Towards an innovative monetary ecosystem to finance a greener tomorrow!'

Moneef R. Zou'bi, PhD, *Science Advisor, InterAction Council (IAC); Co-Founding Director, World Sustainability Forum (WSF)*

'A compelling proposal and a must read for all those who are interested in a system approach for the International monetary system to address peace, stability and inequality'.

Donato Kiniger Passigli, *Vice President & UN Representative, Word Academy of Art and Science*

'A must read for all those who want to understand that one of the most damaging myths of mainstream economics is that money is neutral. Instead it motivates and shapes our economies. Brunnhuber outlines how a new Bretton Woods is needed to create a new monetary architecture for a sustainable future'.

Steve Keen, *Prof. former head of economics, history and politics, Kingston, London*

Financing for Development

This book provides a robust argument for an upgrade of the financial system to enable a more sustainable approach. It explores the upcoming debate on a newly modified international financial architecture, facing serial ecological crisis and the advent of new technologies, which operates in a multipolar world.

Instead of business as usual scenarios, it explores new, innovative, out-of-the-box approaches in the following arenas: taxonomy and regulation, including capital flow management measures and taxations schemas; financial engineering, such as hedging instruments private public partnerships; and polity frameworks, e.g., IMF, World Bank, multilateral development banks and voting quota. It addresses the new role of Central Bank Digital Currencies (CBDCs), the current and upcoming campaign on debt restructuring, as well as the role of new technologies – AI and Blockchain – to tackle illicit financial transactions and fraud, including predictive coding and big DATA correlations. This book focuses on the new role of monetary regulators and central bankers in providing conditioned, additional liquidity to finance, hedge and manage our global commons and to mobilize private capital at the same time, meaning that monetary policy will oversteer fiscal and credit policy in a Bretton Woods II process. The author argues that a new green Bretton Woods 2.0 will provide the agenda to transform our economy and our society, and a Green Transition plan is included in this book.

This will serve as a comprehensive reader for students, scholars and activists in the fields of macroeconomics, international development policy, finance and sustainability. It will also appeal to policy makers and executives in the financial sector as well as informed monetary experts.

Stefan Brunnhuber, MD, PhD, is a trustee at the World Academy of Art and Science and a member of the Club of Rome and endowed chair in sustainability.

Routledge Focus on Economics and Finance

The fields of economics are constantly expanding and evolving. This growth presents challenges for readers trying to keep up with the latest important insights. Routledge Focus on Economics and Finance presents short books on the latest big topics, linking in with the most cutting-edge economics research. Individually, each title in the series provides coverage of a key academic topic, whilst collectively the series forms a comprehensive collection across the whole spectrum of economics.

Reading John Maynard Keynes
A Short Introduction
Andrés Solimano

Regional Economic Integration in East Asia
Institutions, Agreements and the European Experience
Magdalena Suska

Capital Structure and Firm Performance
Global Financing Decisions among Listed Companies
Ewelina Sokołowska and Milad Zargartalebi

Health insurance in the United States of America
Austrian Perspectives on Interventionism before ObamaCare
Łukasz Jasiński

Financing for Development
Towards a New, Green Bretton Woods
Stefan Brunnhuber

For more information about this series, please visit: www.routledge.com/Routledge-Focus-on-Economics-and-Finance/book-series/RFEF

Financing for Development

Towards a New, Green Bretton Woods

Stefan Brunnhuber

Routledge
Taylor & Francis Group
LONDON AND NEW YORK

First published 2025
by Routledge
4 Park Square, Milton Park, Abingdon, Oxon OX14 4RN

and by Routledge
605 Third Avenue, New York, NY 10158

Routledge is an imprint of the Taylor & Francis Group, an informa business

British Library Cataloguing-in-Publication Data
A catalogue record for this book is available from the British Library

Library of Congress Cataloging-in-Publication Data
Names: Brunnhuber, Stefan author
Title: Financing for development : towards a new, green bretton woods / Stefan Brunnhuber.
Description: Abingdon, Oxon ; New York, NY : Routledge, 2025. |
Series: Routledge focus on economics and finance | Includes bibliographical references and index.
Identifiers: LCCN 2025005130 (print) | LCCN 2025005131 (ebook) |
ISBN 9781032814612 hbk | ISBN 9781032814629 pbk |
ISBN 9781003499978 ebk
Subjects: LCSH: Finance | Sustainability | Banks and banking, Central
Classification: LCC HG173 .B78 2025 (print) | LCC HG173 (ebook) |
DDC 332—dc23/eng/20250416
LC record available at https://lccn.loc.gov/2025005130
LC ebook record available at https://lccn.loc.gov/2025005131

ISBN: 978-1-032-81461-2 (hbk)
ISBN: 978-1-032-81462-9 (pbk)
ISBN: 978-1-003-49997-8 (ebk)

DOI: 10.4324/9781003499978

Typeset in Times New Roman
by codeMantra

Contents

Boxes

Tables

Figures

About the author

Professor Stefan Brunnhuber, MD, PhD, is a psychiatrist, chief medical officer and endowed chair in sustainability. He is a trustee of the World Academy of Art and Science and a member of the European Academy of Sciences and Arts, the Club of Rome and the German Liberal Party (FDP) and currently serves on the German government's Sustainable Finance committee. He has over 500 publications and lectures to his name and more than 25 years of hands-on experience in the fields of finance and sustainability. Contact: www.stefan-brunnhuber.de

Preface

Outside the box

In the preface, I explain the relevance of an outside-the-box approach that emphasises the role of the international monetary system (IMS). The monetary system is, I argue, the most overlooked and powerful tool for social development.

As we face historically unprecedented challenges, are we ready to think and act outside the box? That seems to be the question of our time. Academic greenfield projects and sandbox experiments are not without value. But we need to go further: we need a new mental infrastructure[1] to better understand and grasp the overall complexity that lies ahead. It is intuitive, automatic even, to recognise that money matters. But it takes additional mental effort to realise that we need to stop looking in the rear-view mirror and instead dare to look forward – towards an ever more complex and uncertain future.

The IMS has great potential to help the world community transition to a greener, more balanced future. Yet that potential has been almost entirely overlooked and there is no inflection point in sight. There are reams of discussions and publications on the importance of new technologies, governance systems and lifestyle changes, but while these things are all necessary, they are not enough by themselves. The IMS does not function like a neutral thermometer that simply measures the temperature (which here means capital and commodity prices). Rather, apart from education, it is probably the most powerful social mechanism that humans have ever invented. It has made it possible to coordinate billions of people and trillions of transactions every day, transforming our society and affecting all of us for good or ill. It is no exaggeration to say that whether we destroy our planet or create a better future depends to a very great degree on the design and architecture of the IMS. The IMS is not a panacea, but all aspects of a green global transformation depend in some way or other on an upgraded IMS that is more inclusive, balanced and effective.

We should stop letting wishful thinking determine our conclusions and instead refer to empirical findings and to the political realities that will shape the course of the near future. That is what this book sets out to do.

Note

1 On the concept of 'mental infrastructure' and its application in the sociology of ecology, see Welzer 2011.

1 Introduction

Tomorrow is now

The international monetary system (IMS) is the unquestioned common ground for all economic activities. That is true both in democracies and autocracies, in open societies and failed states and in free-market systems and planned economies. Even terrorist groups, black-market actors and the informal sector use or misuse the IMS in some way or other, or at least depend on it.[1] When delegates from 43 countries met at the Mount Washington Hotel in Bretton Woods, New Hampshire, in July 1944, they embraced a new spirit and mindset, and set new rules that would determine the course of the world economy in the post-war era up until the 1970s. Bretton Woods stands metaphorically for a collective project involving at least three main aspects.[2]

First, *international collaboration*: agreements on common rules were considered to be beneficial for all parties. Even non-binding, 'light-touch' rules were, it was felt, better than taking ad hoc decisions in times of crisis or having nothing in place at all.

Second, a search for a set of *monetary mechanisms* that would enable the real economy to better adjust for trade imbalances, including (a) *capital controls* that permit governments to insulate and protect domestic markets to some extent and give them scope to meet their own targets; and (b) *pegged but adjustable* currencies to reduce economic instability and the volatility of the currencies involved.

Third, the implementation of *new monetary institutions*, in particular the World Bank Group (for financing reconstruction and development projects) and the International Monetary Fund (IMF) (for harmonising international policy and providing assistance to countries that encounter challenges with their balance of payments); attempts were also made to establish an International Trade Organization, but those plans did not come to fruition till the 1990s with the founding of the World Trade Organization.

In this book, I will not discuss whether what we might call 'Bretton Woods 1.0' was a success or not. Rather, my aim is to take the spirit of the Bretton Woods agenda and apply it to the situation we find ourselves in in the third decade of this new millennium. I will not argue for or against the traditional measures implemented under the Bretton Woods agenda, but rather make the

DOI: 10.4324/9781003499978-1

case for a substantial upgrade of the three aspects described above in order to meet the specific challenges that human societies are facing today: serial ecological crises[3] and the emergence of new disruptive technologies, all embedded within the new power games of an increasingly fragile and multipolar world.[4]

With the suspension of gold–dollar convertibility in 1971, the Bretton Woods system broke down. The new order that has dominated ever since, encapsulated in the Washington Consensus of 1992,[5] focuses on deregulation of capital inflows and outflows, lower tariffs and taxes and austerity policies to reduce public deficits and public spending.

The situation in the early 21st century represents a kind of Bretton Woods 2.0[6]: on the one hand, a country with a dominant currency and a trade deficit provides the rest of the world with liquidity; on the other, export-driven countries on the periphery run a surplus and accumulate reserve currencies while trading with the country at the centre. After WWII, the country in the centre was the US, with European nations and Japan as exporting countries on the periphery. Now Europe and Japan have been replaced by China and other emerging economies, but the centre has remained the same, thus leaving the underlying rules of the game intact. However, the overall political power game has changed dramatically. This has affected the IMS, making it more fragile, fractured and fragmented. We are now living under a multipolar world order,[7] which goes hand in hand with a multipolar currency system that exceeds the capability of traditional measures and imposes new challenges.[8]

It is important to emphasise that how an economic system functions will depend far more on how it is designed than on the individual economic actors who participate in it, just as a ship's ability to navigate stormy waters will depend far more on its design and engineering than on the skill of its captain, no matter how experienced they might be. In our current system, we have multiple experienced, highly qualified, well-connected actors, but they are constrained and unable to harness their full potential to achieve better, greener, fairer and more resilient economic outcomes.

The fact is that we cannot turn back the clock. In the third decade of the 21st century, we are in a phase of a monetary non-system. This is why I am calling for a new, green Bretton Woods 2.0, which accepts the new reality of ecological crisis, new technologies and a new political power game, and updates the spirit of the initial Bretton Woods idea to reflect this new reality. That means new forms of rule-based international collaboration, new and unorthodox financial engineering mechanisms and new institutional players to manage, hedge and finance it all. We finally need to realise that the IMS is a public good, which serves to mitigate systemic risks. It secures stability over the long term, acts anti-cyclically over the medium term and provides liquidity assistance in the event of emergencies and shocks in the short term.[9] It is not a private enterprise with limited liability, nor a lawless land where anybody can do whatever they want, but a common agenda that we are all enmeshed in, whether we want it or not. And we should avoid blaming individual actors, but instead push for system change that allows those actors to respond appropriately. The IMS in its current form is not efficient but generates asymmetric information, the wrong incentives, irrational herd behaviours and spillovers, lacks transparency, encourages misuse, creates conflicts of interest and incurs costs it cannot cover.

This book is therefore less concerned with political agendas and real economic activities, and more with the underlying financial incentives that enable or enforce those agendas and activities and that, if structured the right way, could change the world.

Notes

1 One possible blueprint for this new, green Bretton Woods system is the Peace of Westphalia, signed in 1648. The treaty established a new international order in which nation states started negotiating their interests regardless of religious differences or ongoing wars. See Kissinger 2014.
2 Eichengreen 2019.
3 See the most recent update from the 'planetary boundaries' research group: Richardson et al. 2023.
4 See Masala 2022; Münkler 2023. A very brief unilateral period followed after 1989, when the Berlin Wall fell and the Tiananmen Square massacre took place in Beijing. The Washington Consensus and the Rio Declaration of 1992 set the course of history for at least two decades. The Washington Consensus was based on the idea that liberalisation, deregulation and privatisation of the economy would automatically lead to more democracy and more open societies. The Rio Declaration called for the richest countries to contribute a 'peace dividend' of 0.7% of GDP to the Global South – a target that they fell woefully short of. The Global North needs to accept that both the Washington Consensus and the Rio Declaration are history and that a completely new agenda is needed to secure prosperity, peace and sustainability. The IMS could play a crucial role in that process.
5 The Washington Consensus established the principles, procedures and institutions that would dominate the Chicago School-inspired neoliberal world order after the end of the Cold War. In particular, it redefined the roles of the IMF and World Bank. This order has eroded over the past three decades, as US power has declined while that of the BRICS+ and G20 countries has grown. See Williamson 2008.
6 Dooley et al. 2004.
7 Entering a multipolar world with five major players – the USA, China, the EU, Russia and India – is changing the playing field. But despite their divergent political agendas, they all operate within the same monetary system. This means that although the IMS is changing, it still remains a common ground or shared framework. See Masala 2022; Münkler 2023.
8 For example, the strict capital controls that the Chinese impose on the yuan, which are incompatible with a free-floating currency regime. See Zhou 2009.
9 This does not inevitably imply the introduction of a global governance system, which will remain a purely theoretical idea that will never escape the confines of political science seminars. Instead, it supports the web-without-a-weaver approach that I attempt to explain in this book.

2 Finding the right narrative

The many relevant stories we could tell

How is the behaviour of large cohorts of people determined and coordinated? Not by data, but by the interpretation of data; not by events, but by a comprehensive understanding of events.[1] This seems to be true for society as a whole, and for economics and finance in particular. In order to set a new, green Bretton Woods agenda for a new global monetary architecture, we need an underlying narrative that we can all agree on. In this book, I take a systemic view of the IMS that incorporates interdisciplinary and empirical findings to interpret the reality around us. The map is not the territory and the menu is not the meal, but a good map can help us navigate better and a good menu can help us find the right meal.[2] Or to choose a different metaphor: if we're sitting in the bottle, we can't read the label. A systemic approach can make that possible.[3]

By contrast with 1944, our current situation is first and foremost characterised by serial asymmetric shocks due to multiple ecological crises. Much has been written about it, and public attention is focused on heatwaves, climate change, forced migration, biodiversity loss, plastic waste and desertification, to name just a few issues. Regular empirical updates and scientific reports tell us more about the state of the planet. They confirm that we are on the wrong path and constantly overshooting planetary boundaries.[4]

But the role of the monetary system has been widely neglected. From a purely financial perspective, all these multiple ecological crises simply represent additional costs, prosperity losses in the near and far future and political instability and the collateral costs associated with it – regardless of which region we are living in and which political agenda we favour. That means the ecological crisis we are witnessing affects all of us, albeit in an asymmetric manner. Some will be hit harder and sooner, others later. Some will escape more or less unscathed and a few will even benefit from it in the short term. But none of us know which side of the story we are on.[5] We have already caused the damage, the risks, the adverse events, and we are starting to experience all the negative impacts. Now we have to come up with a strategy that reduces the associated future costs, keeping global warming and the loneliness that comes with biodiversity loss to a minimum. That requires a secondary

DOI: 10.4324/9781003499978-2

preventive approach to finance: instead of preventing damage (since we have caused it already), we need to identify monetary incentives that will help us to reduce the predicted soaring costs that lie ahead and adapt successfully.[6] And we are forced to rethink the future timeline, taking intergenerational and transnational aspects into consideration. In short: if we outsource the costs to future generations, the Global South or nature in general and continue business as usual, the overall bill will be staggeringly expensive. And the longer we wait, the even more expensive it will be.[7] Finally, given all the external social and ecological shocks ahead, we need an overarching monetary framework that enables not just monetary mechanisms that respond anti-cyclically to the boom-and-bust cycles we are already familiar with, but monetary adaptation mechanisms that allow us to mitigate and minimise the cost avalanche ahead.

The second part of the narrative that differs from 1944 is that the political battlefield has substantially changed. The bipolar world of 1945–1989 has given way to a multipolar one. Brazil is the largest biodiversity power, India is the largest democracy with the highest growth rates, China is the largest state-capitalist economy with the largest public infrastructure programme (Belt and Road Initiative), the EU is one of the largest regulated and socially balanced economies and the US is the largest fossil fuel producer, military power and economy. New mid-sized powers like Saudi Arabia, South Africa, Nigeria, Indonesia and Mexico will further reshape the landscape and give rise to shifting coalitions.

We are living in a multipolar moment, which requires adjustments to our monetary agreements and mechanisms. Simply pursuing controls for footloose capital, utilising pegged and adjustable currencies and allowing the World Bank Group to finance disaster management ex post will not be enough and will clearly be too expensive for all of us. The world of the 2020s is different from that of 75 years ago. While 20 years ago the G7 constituted over 45% of global GDP and the BRICS countries just under 19%, recent figures from the World Bank show the gap is shrinking. Table 2.1 breaks down the first-order macroeconomic data.[8]

The BRICS+ countries represent a diverse range of political agendas and alternately form coalitions for and against the G7. Table 2.1 shows that while they still have less economic power than the G7 states, they have over five times the population, three times the expected growth rate, a similar enrolment rate and higher rates of innovation and patents. At the same time, BRICS+ countries are vastly underrepresented in the voting quotas of relevant international financial institutions (World Bank and IMF), though their relative position is set to improve due to the economic catching-up process.

Below, I will analyse that process in more detail. Economic power can generate a positive-sum game, in which free and fair trade can yield benefits for everyone. Political power in the international system, by contrast, is ultimately a zero-sum game. One party's relative net gain always translates into a relative loss for another. The stronger the BRICS+ countries become, the

Table 2.1 The multipolar moment: BRICS+ versus G7

	G7	*BRICS+*
Population[a]	772 mill.	3,590 mill.
Share of global GDP[a]	43%	28%
GDP/capita (PPP)[a]	50,969 USD	2,603 USD
Public debt/GDP[b]	126%	79%
GINI[a]	0.33	0.40
Unemployment rate[a]	5.3%	6.1%
Military expenditure/GDP[a]	2.7%	2.0%
Healthcare/GDP[a]	13%	5%
Education/GDP[a]	4.8%	3.9%
Foreign direct investment/GDP[a]	2.7%	0.3%
Expected growth rate[d]	1.3%	3.9%
Voting quota in UN[e]	3.6%	5.2%
Voting quota in WTO[e]	4.2%	6.1%
Voting quota in WB[h]	38.96%	11.4%
Voting quota in IMF[e]	41%	18%
Inflation rate[a]	6.6%	3.0%
Five-year child mortality[a]	4.8 per 1,000	20.5 per 1,000
Life expectancy[a]	81 years	74 years
Enrolment rate[a]	98.4%	98.2%
High-volume currency trading[f]	138.7%	11.3%
Patents/y[a]	578,468	1,411,252
Scientific publications/y[a]	989,532	1,097,056
Start-ups[g]	87,431	21,767
Corruption index[a]	1.3	−0.3
Carbon footprint[a]	0.18 kg per USD	0.39 kg per USD

G7: Canada, Germany, France, UK, Italy, Japan, USA plus EU; BRICS+: Brazil, Russia, India, China, South Africa, Egypt, Ethiopia, Iran, Saudi Arabia, UAE, further explanations and sources of a-e see footnote 8

weaker the G7 will be. And the longer the G7 waits, the weaker its political bargaining power to transform international institutions and influence trade and currency regimes. The psychological framings of our political and economic narratives determine whether we end up with a positive or zero-sum game. For example, there is no reason to assume that the BRICS+ countries will continue to rely on the dollar-based SWIFT system rather than building up their own currency exchange system over time or supporting a monetary ecosystem that further weakens the existing IMS and the G7.[9] We can confidently expect the world to be completely different in ten years from now, dominated by alternating political alliances that do not fully conform to the Western narrative. And the longer everyone waits, the more unstable and volatile the overall situation will be for both the G7 and BRICS+ countries. One possible scenario is that the G7 lose relative negotiating power over the coming years due to the BRICS+ countries catching up, while the BRICS+ countries struggle disproportionately with increasing social and ecological externalities and political instability compared with the G7. For example, the costs of ecological crises affecting countries around the equator are up to five times higher than in other places.[10] So both parties have an intrinsic interest in an adjusted IMS that factors in both trade-offs: the relative loss of power and the absolute costs of ecological damage and political instability.

This is the *multipolar moment* we are in right now.[11] An unstable, hybrid, transitional period, in which global challenges and national interests will further converge and alternating alliances will become increasingly unpredictable. Each country on its own is too small to fund, hedge and manage these challenges. At the same time the instruments and tools we have used in the past lack the scale and speed needed to tackle the hazards we are facing today. No country, no institution, no one agenda and no technology can yet claim that it has found a way to master the crises that lie ahead.

Ignoring the bigger picture will leave each country worse off. Instead of advocating for global governance (which is not going to happen any time soon), we should aim for a common agenda that accounts for both conflicting national interests and common global challenges. The IMS is a perfect candidate for implementing such an agenda. And instead of aiming solely for additional charity, global taxation, philanthropy and overseas development aid (though all these things have their benefits), that agenda should take the form of an updated and upgraded Bretton Woods agenda.[12] Meaning that instead of focusing on corporate investments, political agendas or consumer patterns, we should prioritise institutional incentives: polity over politics and practices. I will outline the main elements of my proposed agenda in the next chapters.

If we take the biophysical reality and the scientific imperative, with all its overshoots and backlashes, as a given, and consider the uninspiring results we have achieved so far, we can see that the overall situation is becoming seriously complex: on the one hand, the G7 countries are better prepared to tackle the ecological crisis than the BRICS+ ones; but on the other, overall economic power is shifting towards the BRICS+ states. In short, the Global South will be more affected by the climate crisis than the Global North, but the North is losing its institutional power and its unique leverage to cope with the situation. This dilemma will force both the G7 and BRICS+ countries to join forces on monetary and environmental policy.

If we turn back our attention to the past, the initial idea, expressed in the Washington Consensus and Rio Declaration of 1992, was that a free, privatised and deregulated market would ultimately lead to more democracy and open societies and that a 'peace dividend' would create a more peaceful and sustainable future for the world. That has proved to be wishful thinking. In 2020, 47% of the world's population are living in non-democratic regimes or failed states,[13] while biodiversity loss, global warming and deforestation are soaring like there's no tomorrow. And since the success of the ecological transformation will mainly be decided in the Global South and requires a systemic solution, we need to find systems or mechanisms that can deliver that solution. The IMS is one of them. The new clash of political systems, between open societies on the one hand and autocracies on the other, will therefore force us to rethink processes of international collaboration between countries with diverse political agendas. We cannot expect that in the near future countries like Russia or China will convert to open societies on a Western model. In a world where everything is connected with everything else and we are forced to deal with ongoing ecological crises, a new, greener and universally accepted IMS is required so that we can rethink the rules of the game, instead of simply adjusting the existing ones to allow greater efficiency and ad hoc collaborations.

In addition to the ecological challenges and the increasingly multipolar world order, there is a third development that will affect all countries and have a significant impact on the IMS: the dawn of new digital technologies, in particular AI, synthetic biology, robotics and quantum computing. These technologies will, first, affect the way financial transactions are carried out. New innovations in fintech will radically change the landscape of commercial banking, money creation, liabilities and business. Second, these innovations will have a substantial impact on international power games. The country with the first quantum AI computing will set the new rules of the game. Third, these new technologies will attract investors and determine the future flows of capital. The course of any sustainable future and any multilateral agreement is dependent on them. I have dedicated a separate chapter to this topic.

The narrative I have sketched above should motivate a shared, mission-based agenda,[14] where projects determine the financial needs instead of finance driving our sustainability agenda. Such a mission-based approach would, ideally, not only build on international trade, reconstruction and development but go beyond them to create peace, security and sustainability for all. We need an agenda that is able to reconcile national interests and international resources, micro and macro perspectives, environmental and economic factors, East and West, North and South, private and public, all with the aim of greater balance. An agenda with anti-cyclical, built-in stabilisers that can respond to external shocks and that permits a long-term perspective that looks beyond short-term boom-and-bust cycles. An agenda that encourages us to transcend conflicting political systems and cultural differences and move towards a multilateralism that can address intergenerational issues and the associated responsibilities.

The deregulation, privatisation and liberalisation that have defined the process of globalisation since 1992 originated in the idea of a fair and competitive market mechanism. But just as antibiotic resistance did not convince us to abandon antibiotics, but to make them better, social and ecological externalities, the formation of oligopolies and unfair information asymmetries should not lead us to abandon market mechanisms, but rather to rebuild them to increase political stability and peace, economic prosperity and resilience (beyond ad hoc facilities), social inclusion and well-being and ecological

Table 2.2 Elements of a new narrative for any future IMS

Reconstruction and development	Eastern and Western narratives
Multipolarity (G7 versnus BRICS+)	Integrating North and South
Multilateralism and multiculturalism	Integrating micro and macro
Intergenerational	Systems thinking and autopoiesis
Anti-cyclical and external shocks	New technologies, multidisciplinarity, science-based
Price signals and market instability	Private goods and global commons
A web without a weaver	State and market
National interest and global resources	Sovereignty and responsibility
Mission-based: peace, security, sustainability	Mission drives finance, rather than finance driving mission
Freedom and responsibility	Boundaries and biophysical limits

longevity. We would then enter a green transition period that utilises the benefits of price signals while acknowledging that markets remain inherently unstable.[15] And we would then be able to de-risk, hedge and mobilise private capital and to fund and manage global commons all at the same time.

The challenge, then, is to translate the narrative I have outlined into a comprehensive IMS. We should not be satisfied with anything less – and only an agenda that meets these ambitions deserves the title of a new, green Bretton Woods agenda. Table 2.2 summarises some elements that agenda would need to include.

A new, green IMS would need to be largely agnostic with regards to overall economic activity in the real economy and capital market and the underlying political agenda, except for three elements. First, it should provide monetary tools to cope with inflationary pressure and price instability due to the expected rises in energy and food prices and the growing instability and volatility of the capital market. Second, it should offer a monetary toolkit that supports national policies to prevent mass unemployment in an age of disruptive technologies. Third, it should account for the stressors on our environment. Whereas the first two points align with traditional ways of looking at monetary policy, the third makes reference to (global) ecological commons.[16] From a financial perspective, it seems irrational to assume that nation states and their policies will be able to tackle global commons and their associated negative collective externalities by themselves. It seems to be next to impossible to redirect responsibility for global ocean waste, massive biodiversity loss, water pollution, climate-related flooding or extreme weather to nation states, companies or individual behavioural and lifestyle changes alone. Almost 80% of the entire global value chain is still deeply ingrained in fossil energy. Extractors of oil and gas, manufacturers of fossil derivatives worldwide and global consumers are jointly causing these negative collective externalities. We made the mess together, and so we have to come up with a problem-solving strategy together too. Imagining we could re-privatise or personalise these collective externalities is like thinking we could put toothpaste back once it's already out of the tube.

Notes

1 This primarily refers to humans' selection advantage. See Harari 2014 and Shiller 2019.

2 Our choice of economic narrative determines how we interpret economic data. If we choose a mechanistic approach, we will get machine-like results. And depending on whether we choose a microeconomic, institutional, game-theoretic, Marxist or Keynesian approach, we will get different and often conflicting stories about the same event. This book's narrative is guided by a systems theory approach that integrates interdisciplinary findings.

3 Instead of advocating solely for a loss and damage fund for the Global South, which remains a noble and necessary goal, we should aim for the higher goal of resetting the framework of the monetary system itself. See Climate Analytics 2023.

4 On planetary boundaries, see Richardson et al. 2023. We are now living on a hot (global warming) and lonely (biodiversity loss) planet, where almost 50% of the world population is directly affected and vulnerable (harvest defaults, water stress, forced migration) and the other 50% indirectly (stranded assets, disruption of value chains, political instability). See IPCC 2023.

5 There is a rich literature on ecological effects on humans in the Anthropocene. For reviews of this literature, see McDonald 2018; Uexkull and Buhaug 2021; Adger et al. 2022; Issa et al. 2023.

6 In public health literature, a distinction is drawn between primary prevention, where we avoid the damage in the first place; secondary prevention, where we try to minimise the costs of the damage; and tertiary prevention, where we try to deal with long-term, irreversible damage. The sooner we intervene, the cheaper it will be. See Kisling and Das 2023.

7 This kind of non-linear relationship between effort and effect is well known (see for instance Pareto's law) and corresponds to the fat-tailed distributions that are characteristic of complex systems. There is a vast body of empirical literature on project management and cost overruns that shows how excessive overrun is a common challenge for managing complex systems. See Flyvbjerg et al. 2018 and Flyvbjerg and Gardner 2024.

8 The data comprises weighted averages (weighted for GDP and population). Sources:

a – Data from World Bank 2023 (population – 2019; GDP and GDP/capita – 2022; Gini index – 2019, except for South Africa (2014) and Ethiopia (2015); unemployment rate as percentage of total labour force modelled by ILO – 2021; military expenditure – 2022 for G7, 2021 for BRICS+, except Saudi Arabia (2014); healthcare/GDP (% of GDP) – 2018; education/GDP – 2020; foreign direct investment net outflows as percentage of GDP – 2022; inflation rate – 2022; five-year child mortality rate – 2019; life expectancy – 2019; enrolment rate – 2016 for G7, 2010 for BRICS+; patent applications and residents – 2020; scientific publications/year – 2020; CO_2 emissions per USD PPP of GDP – 2019; controls on corruption – 2019)

b – Data from IMF for 2023 (see IMF Datamapper 2023)

c – Data from Statista for 2024 (very similar outlook for 2025 to 2028)

d – Own calculation based on member states and voting formula

e – Data from the Bank for International Settlements for 2022. Euro shares for France, Italy and Germany calculated by weighting the total euro trading volume according to the country's share of EU GDP; note that the total is 200% since each currency trade is counted twice (purchase and sale) f – Data from the most recent Startup Ranking (2024); number of current start-ups by country

g – Data for 2024 from the World Bank's International Development Association

A special note regarding 'share of global GDP': the charts from Statista (and some press articles) seem to be wrong since the World Bank (Worldometer 2024) and the IMF data visualised on Visual Capitalist in 2023 show a clear gap between G7 and BRICS+ countries of at least 12%.

9 In fact, we can already witness a shift. The EU introduced a multilateral barter system called INSTEX (Instrument in Support of Trade Exchanges) to get around US sanctions; China has CIPS (Cross-Border Interbank Payment System), which includes its own e-payment systems (UnionPay and Alipay); India has UPI (Unified Payments Interface) and MOSIP (Modular Open-Source Identification Platform), which between them already cover over 80% of domestic transactions; and Russia has an alternative to SWIFT in the form of SPFS (Financial Messaging System) and the Mir e-payment system.

10 Persaud 2024.

11 Münkler 2023; Braveboy-Wagner 2024.

12 Such an agenda would also need to factor in colonialism and its history. The forms and structures of colonialism changed over time. Direct land grabs and slavery gave way to unfair, unsustainable trade agreements. The net global outflow of money from the Global South to the Global North every year amounts to ten trillion USD, leaving emerging markets always behind the curve. These loss and damage expenditures are about 30 times greater than overseas development aid (ODA; see Hickel et al. 2022). The Global North's wealth model is primarily responsible for the climate change the Global South has to endure. Forced migration will in turn encourage right-wing nationalists to reject climate action, which will further increase the global imbalance. A green, updated Bretton Woods 2.0 is needed to address this inconvenient truth. See also Chakrabasty 2021; Volz et al. 2024.

13 See Our World in Data 2023.

14 Mazzucato 2021.

15 Under the current market rules, prices do not reflect real underlying values. This is true for the price of money, where the interest rate should reflect an adequate risk premium, the price of goods and services, which should internalise the multiple social and ecological spillovers, and the price of labour, which should accord with minimum wage laws. The reach of free and competitive market allocation should match the reach of the legislation that enables market allocation in the first place. Most of the oft-described externalities are thus not signs of market failure, but rather of a lack of a proper competitive market.

16 Even within the existing mandate and regulatory framework of central banks, which focus solely on price stability (CPI), unemployment and environmental issues will sooner or later translate into a long-term inflationary wage-price spiral. Meaning that even if central banks refuse to extend their mandate beyond the CPI, ensuring long-term price stability is still their job. I will further elaborate on this argument in the following chapters.

3 The traditional way

End of pipe

The systems approach: beyond fractured economics

When we take stock of the dozens of economic theories currently available to us, the first step should be to appreciate their wisdom, while recognising their flaws. None of them is 100% wrong; all of them provide relevant but fragmented knowledge that they claim can be generalised for economic activity as a whole. Traditional economics uses longitudinal measures, such as GDP or unemployment rates, field studies and experiential or historical data in order to look into the future. No traditional economic theory is able to grasp the international monetary system (IMS) as a complex system or network, or to see and evaluate the risks and uncertainties that are intrinsic to such a complex system, nor to substantially question the design and architecture of the IMS itself. Meaning they leave the monetary system untouched and unquestioned, and treat it as a given.[1] In a more general sense, traditional economics fails to answer the simple but non-trivial question: *how can we finance our common future in the face of uncertainties and future shocks in a multipolar world?*

The second step is to take this argument one stage further and apply a systems approach that incorporates interdisciplinary evidence[2] and looks at the IMS as a complex open-flow and network system.[3] We will then be able to see that the challenges ahead are not cyclical in nature, but non-linear and disruptive, following an S-curve rather than a straight line, and that we are confronted with massive collective externalities and future cost and damage functions that go far beyond the traditional growth trajectory of 2–3% globally. In numbers: the post-WWII European recovery plan known as the Marshall Plan[4] represented roughly 5% of US GDP, the EU eastern enlargement about 0.1–0.2% of EU GDP, the Rio Declaration of 1992 to fund the Global South 0.8% of global GDP and German reunification about 74 billion euros annually (in 2019 prices), equivalent to roughly 1.5% of German GDP in 1991.[5] Even when the Comecon and Eastern Europe's planned economy collapsed, ushering in a competitive market economy, the rules of the game were already known and in place. The amount of money required for the systems change needed in the 21st century is about eight to ten times higher than

DOI: 10.4324/9781003499978-3

any historical precedent. We have to transform an entire energy system along a global value chain and restore nature at the same time while facing unprecedented social and ecological externalities; we can no longer ignore these costs and are forced to operate in an opaque political environment where the line between allies and enemies is constantly shifting. Rather than applying the existing monetary rules to a new historical situation, we need to come up with new ones that allow us to globally reframe the entire underlying energy system, fund our global commons, enable emerging new technologies to scale up and be made accessible to all and provide the tools needed to mobilise trillions of private-sector funding for our common future. There is no real historical blueprint we can draw on. And this time the change has to be applied to ourselves, to our own political agenda, to our own business and our own day-to-day private lives. It is like a marathon runner performing surgery on their own heart in the middle of a race using a new and not yet fully proven method. The paradigm shift from a fossil to a renewable era alone will require at least 7–10% of GDP each year, surpassing all growth trajectories of the past. We must admit that we caused the damage in the first place and need to adopt a secondary preventive approach and new rules of the game in order to lower future costs. This systems approach will encourage us to move beyond well-known academic rituals and activism and to dance with this complex open network system instead of pretending to control it (Box 3.1).[6]

Box 3.1 Systems thinking in finance

A closer look: a systems approach to finance means that the input, while sensitive, does not wholly determine the output; all variables are interconnected and analysis of historical data cannot account for the scope, magnitude and dynamics of all future outcomes and risks; complex does not equal complicated; irreversible tipping points, fatality events, emergent structures and multicausality are becoming the new normal; finance as an open, complex system has a tendency towards self-organisation and butterfly effects, with fuzzy and hybrid logics dominating over clarity and clear-cut prognostic results; scale-independent fractals, attractors and a helicopter view are better able to describe the systems dynamic than any linear thinking; none of this is accessible by the naked eye, Excel sheets and best academic guesses.

TRAPP: finance still drives our future

Within the current monetary regime, our opportunities and risks are mainly driven by finance. It is the financial system that determines whether or not investments are made and projects completed. If there is no money available, opportunities such as new jobs, technological innovation, universal healthcare, infrastructure programmes and education will simply not be utilised, even if the need for these things is obvious. Even if we have the brightest ideas and unambiguous scientific evidence, the existence of the challenges is undisputed and there are needs that are wholly unmet, it is ultimately finance that will determine whether or not these ideas meet the criteria of the profit floor or are simply abandoned. The same is true for risk assessment. If there is no funding available, companies will not invest in an uncertain environment and will reduce their commitment to searching for new drugs for cancer or infectious diseases, while governmental bodies will avoid implementing the necessary policies for infrastructure programmes.[7] There are at least five measures that dominate the current financial regime, which I collectively refer to as TRAPP:

- Taxation.
- Restructuring loans and debts.
- Austerity measures.
- Privatisation.
- Philanthropy.

Transferring money through fees and taxation

In a general sense, taxes, fees and subsidies represent each citizen's and company's explicit relation to the state as well as the implicit relations between citizens and companies. Both sets of relations together represent a legal agreement on how to redistribute, manage and fund economic activities, wealth and public infrastructure.[8] But *funding* is just one of the four major reasons why taxation schemes are in place. *Managing consumption patterns* (sin tax) and *investment behaviours* (landmines, coal mines), *tackling inflation* (especially for food and energy) and *maintaining social cohesion* by addressing intolerable income and wealth gaps are the others. We will see that the funding that they generate is far too slow and low in volume to meet the challenges we are facing. The entire global tax intake reflects the fiscal effort of collecting money from ongoing economic activities in the private sector. In 2023 global tax intake represented about 14% of global GDP, or roughly 15 trillion USD.[9] Although rich countries represented in the Organisation for Economic Co-operation and Development (OECD) countries can rely on a broad tax base, including a variety of taxation schemes, emerging economies have a tax base that is 80% smaller. That is despite great heterogeneity in global tax structures and a general tendency towards international convergence, which all depends on the domestic tax base, income per capita, the openness and composition of the economy and external debt load. The proportion of transfer payments ranges from 10 to 45% of domestic GDP.[10] There are dozens of carefully designed taxation schemes and a lively academic and social debate on how to refinance social and ecological goods and services, tackle negative externalities and fund our commons. Progressive income taxation, wealth and inheritance taxes and Valued Added Tax (VAT) are the most prominent suggestions. These methods do have some value but are chronically difficult to realise in a democratic political system. Given that the poorest 10% of Scandinavian citizens are richer than the average Polish worker, and that private wealth of about 5,000 USD already qualifies someone as belonging to the upper 50% of the world population, the well-established and conventional way of redistributing money through taxation, fees and subsidies may be one political tool among others, but it does not have the ability, volume or scope to finance our future as a whole. The political and academic debate over the last 75 years has demonstrated the intellectual power of such an approach but also its limits. An inherent paradox of taxation is becoming obvious: in SMEs, over 95% of any earning before income and taxation (EBITA) is reinvested in the firm itself – it is spent on jobs, research and development, new investment and transition measures. Withdrawing that money from the value chain and then reinvesting it seems to be a kind of paradox. Such paradoxes are created when we want to do good and avoid harm, but end up achieving the exact opposite. If, say, a nation responsible for 5% of global atmospheric CO_2 emissions decided to exit the fossil age, the corresponding drop in demand for fossil fuel would trigger a decrease in its price, which in turn would very likely increase consumption in other parts of the world. This 'green paradox'[11] is a dilemma for any good that is tradable on a global scale. Any activity to reduce dependency on fossil energy is valid only as long as the CO_2 remains in the ground. As long as there are insufficient equivalent alternative investments available, reducing fossil consumption unilaterally is logically counterproductive. What is more, any rational producer of fossil energy will actually be incentivised to over-extract their resources in the short term in order to maximise their portfolio and reinvest the revenue elsewhere. Solely relying on VAT or corporate, capital and inheritance taxes is an ineffective and inefficient way to fund, hedge and manage the transition.[12] It's like pulling on both sides of a tablecloth, and in the end achieving little to nothing. After the government has taxed the rich, it still needs the private sector again to do the job of implementing renewables, building hospitals and nursing homes and providing new technologies for the transition. One of the clearest signs that the entire IMS is systemically flawed is the mismatch between direct and indirect subsidies for damaging our planet on the one hand and funding measures for conservation and restoration of nature on the other. The former amounts to seven trillion USD, the latter to a mere 80 to 150 billion.[13] If we continue to invest 500 times more in destroying our natural world than in preserving it, the outcome should be obvious to everybody. In order to bridge the gap and fund our transition, we would need to increase global tax intake by 50%. All taxation schemes are end-of-pipe strategies, where we do whatever we want first and then tax the results and try to do good second. No OECD country is yet capable of generating enough liquidity through tax intake to cover the global externalities and fund our future. In sum, taxation is part of the solution, but it is not *the* solution.

Restructuring loans

Debt has become a double-edged sword. On the one hand, if investment is targeted correctly, it can provide future opportunities, while loans and a balanced burden between the generations are vital for development and a transition towards a more sustainable future; on the other hand, debt can be a curse, especially if the investment was a mismatch and/or the repayment schemes undermine investments in key sectors, such as healthcare, education or infrastructure, where the growth rate of debt is outpacing GDP.[14] Servicing the debt load or serving the people has become an unresolved dilemma for governments representing almost half of the world's population. We are confronted with a global debt burden of almost 1000 trillion USD, made up of borrowing by governments (2/5) and borrowing by businesses and households (3/5). 80% of that total has been generated by rich OECD countries. However, it is the countries of the Global South,[15] especially developing nations, that suffer the most from their debt curse, due to uneven access to additional liquidity and private capital as well as higher borrowing costs. Currently, over 100 countries have been forced to cut their spending on education, social protection and healthcare because of increased interest rates and repayments. Low-income households are most affected by the lack of public services and risk falling back into poverty.[16] Empirical evidence shows that any economy that is subject to stress, uncertainty and increasing shocks will generate additional private-sector debt, creating a need for additional credit lines provided by those who have enough liquidity. This 'rich glut' further widens the income and wealth gap, which forces the public sector to ultimately cover the additional costs by taking on further debt.[17]

However, the devil is in the detail.[18] We can identify six major sources of loans for developing countries: private lenders; China; other bilateral agencies; the Paris Club; multilateral development banks (MDBs); and the World Bank's international development assistance. All lenders follow their own agendas. Private creditors (commercial banks, bondholders and institutional investors) account for two-thirds of total external public debt in developing countries, which makes restructuring of different maturities, grace periods and interest rates and risk spreads more complicated and expensive.[19] In general, developing countries pay substantially more for debt relief relative to GDP than rich OECD countries, which further exacerbates the asymmetry between the Global North and Global South. The main lesson we can learn from history here[20] is that if we wish to return to a path of sustainable economic growth for all, which would help establish a positive-sum game, the minimum required to fairly share the burden would be 0.7% of GDP pledged for overseas development aid, the three to five trillion USD equivalent needed to plug the financial gap and meet the UN Sustainability Development Goals (SDGs)[21] and another 200–300 billion USD annually to cover additional costs for loss and damage due to climate change.[22] It would also be necessary to implement controls on corruption and fraud and harmonise the various restructuring measures. The way debt is currently designed generates an ongoing trade-off between haircuts, additional lending, grants and concessional contracts. Although additional grants and loans will keep debt vulnerability and risk indicators high and fail to attract private investments, debt relief will reduce nominal debt burden and provide more fiscal space to fund public goods, improve risk assessment and allow further private investment to be mobilised.[23]

Despite all these limitations, the general argument still holds: the system as a whole is flawed so that an unmanageable debt burden crowds out public commons; massive liquidity outflows to the Global North cause systemic fiscal tightening; the lack of proper reimbursements for loss and damage leaves billions uncovered and unprotected; and fraud, corruption and tax evasion counteract any attempts to bring about a 'fresh start' and level playing field as we progress towards a common future. Taken together, these factors create a vicious circle that whole countries, regions and even continents cannot escape. This is one of the reasons why James Tobin called debt the Achilles heel of capitalism.[24] The trap is systemic in nature, not solely a matter of individual failures. Only if we are prepared to change systemic incentives can we create a sound basis for future development. In order to make the IMS more inclusive and provide additional liquidity, a debt workout mechanism is required that allows upfront loading, long-term maturities and public guarantees to hedge, fund and manage public interests and to scale up and mobilise private capital investment in volatile and risky environments. I will discuss this mechanism in later chapters.

Austerity policies

Austerity refers to policy measures that seek to cut public spending in order to meet governmental debt obligations and allocate a society's resources more efficiently. Historically, this translated into liberalising, deregulating and privatising our economy.[25] Such efficiency measures are best described as streamlining a system's components and better managing potential throughput per unit. Outsourcing, private investments in R&D, educational programmes, preventing fraud and corruption and implementing new technologies will indeed help us to deploy our resources more effectively and efficiently.[26] And for as long as we waste about a third of our food production, equal to the amount necessary to feed Canada and India combined, there is still a long way to go to make our supply system more efficient. Supporters of austerity argue that reduced (external) debt loads and public deficit spending can help further increase future productivity and output. However, austerity is just one-half of the equation and not an end in itself. Focusing solely on efficiency makes a system more fragile, volatile and unstable.[27] In order to make a system more robust and sustainable, resilience factors first need to be in place. Resilience is the ability to recover from a shock. The resilience of a system is measured by its interconnectedness and the diversity of its mechanisms. A systems approach can demonstrate that the most efficient system is simultaneously the most fragile and volatile. Nature never selected for efficiency, but rather for a sensible balance between throughput (efficiency) and interconnectedness (resilience), with the dominant factor being stability rather than volatility. We can observe the same principle in flight safety, power grids, agricultural monoculture and every ecosystem, and it should be applied to the monetary system too. The two variables, efficiency and resilience, are intertwined.[28] We need to find sensible measures that strike the right balance between efficiency and resilience, placing us in an optimal 'anti-fragile' zone where the system is able to learn from failure and maintain its overall integrity.[29] Anything outside this zone is either too unstable (too efficient) or too stagnant (too resilient). Figure 3.1 illustrates this general point.[30]

More generally speaking, the native human mind is characterised by short-term decisions and flawed mental frames, and operates in the 'middle dimension' of metres and minutes. We are not wired to deal with complexity.[31] This is why humans require cultural achievements like new technologies, coordinated rules of the game and an adjusted monetary system to fill the gap.

Such considerations also apply to austerity measures and the IMS in general, especially given that we are facing increasing volatility and banking, currency, government and debt crises. Financial markets are generally considered to be efficient, self-regulating and decentralised systems for allocating goods and services through price signals, where demand and supply spontaneously converge over a defined maturity. They are seen as one of the most efficient

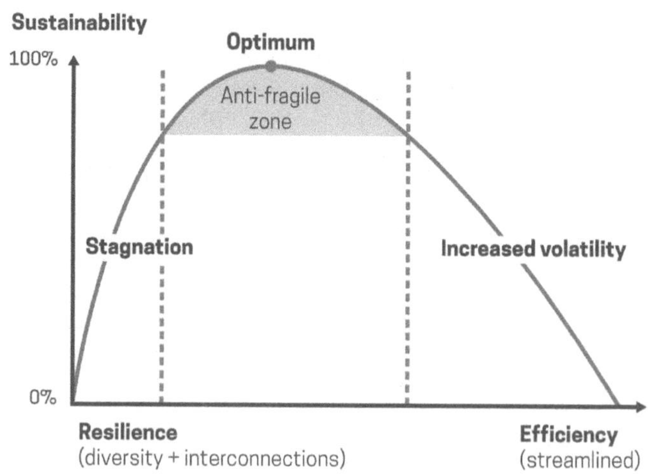

Figure 3.1 Efficiency and resilience: the anti-fragile zone

allocative mechanisms humans ever devised. And they represent probably the largest circular economic process ever invented. Demand on one side of the planet meets supply on the other trillions of times every day, based on price signals and without much governmental regulation. However, these sorts of highly efficient markets are incomplete and unstable and require resilience measures to remain balanced. Only when a system is in an 'anti-fragile' zone will it not merely passively adapt to the environment but instead perfect a systemic response to asymmetric shocks and defaults.[32] This means that anti-fragile features will improve the IMS's performance. In the next chapters, I will outline key measures for a Bretton Woods 2.0 policy that meet the criteria of increased resilience and the 'anti-fragile zone' and go beyond mere fiscal austerity.

Privatisation

Currently, 85% of all global assets are privatised, while 15% are public. The same percentage, 85%, of all investments are private too, which means the private sector dominates.[33] However, trillions of private cash deposits remain unproductive, stock repurchasing programmes surpass R&D budgets and institutional investors are sitting on a carbon bubble that is growing by more than one trillion USD annually,[34] forcing them to write off substantial parts of their assets. These stranded assets do not yet include the challenges of other systemic shocks like biodiversity loss and harvest defaults, serial pandemics, air pollution and mass forced migration.[35] A significant portion of private credit creation has become decoupled from the real economy, lowering economic productivity and inflating the FIRE (finance/insurance/real estate) sector instead. In the face of massive collective externalities and spillovers, unprecedented asymmetric shocks and an ever-growing complexity and interconnectedness, where profits are privatised and losses are socialised, further privatising the system has its limits. The private sector will still lead the way in the transformation, but we should avoid privatising the remaining 15% of our public goods. And we should note that private capital is always pro-cyclical, short-termist and risk-averse. That means a monetary mechanism is needed that allows us to mobilise trillions of investment in long-term, anti-cyclical measures in a risky environment without destroying the very nature of our global commons.

Philanthropy

Philanthropy and charity worldwide account for about one trillion USD annually[36] being put towards good ends. However, the devil is in the detail. First, tax deduction programmes facilitating charity are covered in all countries by the taxpayer, and investments and grants depend on the functionality of the existing system. If there is a bust, the funding phases out. Empirically, charity payments per capita are highest in the lowest-income segments, which further increases the wealth gap and defeats the purpose of charitable giving. In sum, in its current format philanthropy is an indirect subsidy of society, which enables rich individuals and foundations to provide money to whichever social and environmental projects the donor finds most attractive. Giving grants or gifts and supporting others have always been important aspects of our social coexistence. But the idea that we can build an entire transformation process on a gift economy and leave the monetary architecture untouched seems deeply implausible.[37] Table 3.1 presents a more detailed breakdown of the figures for international liquidity assistance and potential annually adjusted global investments.

While it should be acknowledged that there is some overlap between the institutions mentioned above, the figures show that most of the liquidity currently or previously available has either been earmarked already or is not eligible for investment due to the associated risks. In short, we need additional, conditioned, international liquidity assistance to unlock trillions of private-sector investment, to fund and manage our global commons and to scale up new technologies and make them accessible to everyone. But the system in which all these transactions are occurring is itself unstable, fragile, volatile and unprepared to manage future shocks, finance the green transition or cope with the new reality of a multipolar world.[38] It is possible, however, to flip things around: instead of finance driving our future, with all the constraints associated with it, we should start looking for a monetary regime that allows the opposite: one where our future drives finance.

In other words, instead of solely following a traditional model, where we either tax the current value chain, borrow money from the capital market, solicit private investment from companies, rely on philanthropic donations or simply tighten our fiscal efforts in order to finance a greener and fairer future, we should dare to widen our scope. None of these traditional approaches are wrong per se, but they simply lack the speed and scale that our common agenda demands. The conversion rate from a fossil economy to a more circular, decarbonised one is simply too low and the risks and uncertainty too high for the private sector to fully come on board with that agenda.[39] We are overconfident that the existing IMS will fix things, even though irreversible ecological and social tipping points, stranded assets with massive write-offs, the breakdown of entire global value chains, forced migration and political instability will bring with them additional costs that the IMS and domestic budgets will somehow have to manage. In short, the transition we are all going through right now is not a cyclical phenomenon, but a non-linear, disruptive one. It doesn't come for free but has a price tag attached. The longer we wait, the more expensive that price tag will be.[40] And if we refuse to put a price tag on our future and the natural world, we effectively set the price at zero and discount our common future (Box 3.2).[41]

Box 3.2 Climate finance

Take climate change as a case study. Most financial experts and academics agree that a carbon tax is the best steering measure to shift companies, consumers and states away from the fossil age and towards a low-carbon economy. The required carbon pricing should be for each tonne of CO_2 emissions and come to around 200 USD/t. The emissions trading system should run round the clock 365 days a year. Currently (2025), we are able to cover about 25% globally with cap-and-trade and taxation schemes at a much lower price (80 USD/t).[42] A global carbon price would immediately affect all bonds, treasuries, securities, firms and any capital allocation. It should run in shadow form for one to two years and then become real. Minimising the damage associated with climate change will cost up to 5% of global GDP. We can either invest in preventing the damage (primary prevention), adapt to the spillovers (secondary prevention) or repair the damage later on (tertiary prevention) through loss and damage funds. We should be aware that tertiary prevention is by far the most expensive option.[43] The fact of the matter is that the more we are prepared to pay upfront for primary preventive measures, the less we will have to pay for the two others (adaptation and damage control). We currently invest about one trillion USD in climate change measures. But the figure that is needed is around five to seven times higher, which means there will be far higher adaptation and damage costs ahead than ever before. So far, investing in climate mitigation has simply not been sufficiently profitable for the private sector, while governments are constrained in how much funding they can provide and institutional investors have obligations to their constituents (in particular pensions for the baby boomer generation, who number 270 million globally). A rising CO_2 concentration in the atmosphere due to emissions from fossil fuels is a *global negative collective externality*, jointly caused by producers, manufacturers and consumers. Privatising this collective externality through taxonomies and taxation, waiting until the profit floor for companies is suitable and leaving the public sector and regulators out of the equation will be extremely expensive and ineffective. CO_2 emissions are not the result of a global market failure, but rather due to the lack of a suitable competitive market able to provide efficient price signalling and market allocation.

This co-financing strategy is a kind of end-of-pipe approach, something that is common in engineering. We first implement certain technologies, lifestyles, rules and economic activities that cause damage to our environment (e.g., air pollution), then add a filter at the end of that process to prevent

Table 3.1 Estimated breaking down of the figures for international investments and liquidity assistance (own calculation)

Institution/channel/ mechanism	*USD*	*Characteristics and constraints*
IMF	1 trillion	Additional special drawing rights (SDRs) are required, especially for developing countries.
WB Group	80 billion (assets under management)	Chronically underfunded, with a lack of scaling and coordination. There remains an annual funding shortfall of billions of USD every year.
WHO	6–7 billion	Chronically underfunded; massive upfront funding required to meet the public health challenges ahead.
45+ multilateral development banks (MDBs) (including WB)	2 trillion	Multilateral banking; lack of overall coordination, scaling and upfront funding.
450+ development finance institutions (DFIs)	15 billion	Bilateral development banks (non-commercial) provide liquidity for the private sector; reliant on government spending; lack of mandate.
Major central banks (US, China, EU, UK, Japan, etc.)	25 trillion	The money base has primarily (80%) been used to purchase state bonds.
Central bank swap and repo lines	500–800 billion or more	The vast majority of swap and repo lines are reserved for currency exchanges between the major convertible currencies; new swap lines are needed.
Foreign direct investments (FDIs)	1.3 trillion	Private capital is pro-cyclical, short-term and risk-averse, causing crowding-out effects on a domestic level.
Commercial banks	180 trillion	Only operate on the basis of profitable returns and are pro-cyclical.
Institutional investors	190 trillion (assets under management)	Largest single player (50% of all financial assets globally), liabilities to their constituents.
Companies	100 trillion	Climate finance is not profitable; lack of scaling and coordination; average depreciation rate of 10% for replacement investments vis too low.
Venture capital	300–500 billion	Doing good and making profit, but too low in volume, too slow and too volatile to reach a relevant systemic tipping point.

(*Continued*)

Table 3.1 (Continued)

Institution/channel/ mechanism	*USD*	*Characteristics and constraints*
Philanthropy	1 trillion	Doing good, but the amount is too small, and the funds and grants are determined by the donor.
Global public debt	120 trillion	High interest payments and military expenses prevent the public sector from doing its job (infrastructure, education, healthcare).
Shadow banking sector	200 trillion	Unregulated, unhedged, untaxed and volatile.
Global tax intake	15 trillion	14% of world GDP; a 50% increase would be necessary to fund the UN SDGs.
Global fossil subsidies	7 trillion	Direct (20%) and indirect (80%); related to excess public health expenditures

excessive harm. The co-financing strategy follows the same rationale. Traditional finance likewise represents a kind of end-of-pipe strategy, where money is redistributed as required but the current system is kept in place. In short: the economy grows first, then we take a certain amount of money (through tax or fees) from the value chain and redistribute it to social and ecological projects. Figure 3.2 summarises the traditional way of financing our future.

The figure represents the traditional approach to finance (large brown arrow) as an end-of-pipe strategy. We maximise the output first, redistribute second and fund our planetary externalities and common goods third. We distribute about one-third at a domestic level, leaving a small portion to fund, hedge and manage our common future. The informal sector and shadow economy (grey box on the left) push the economy in the wrong direction.

Hedging the system: on unknowns and complexity

To take this argument one step further, we need to distinguish between different forms of the unknown. We tend to like the rewards but not the risks. In a general sense, any hazards, risks and uncertainties are potential adverse events that disrupt our daily routine and represent potential losses associated with doing or not doing something. Although there will never be a zero-risk world and all hazards are intertwined, from a financial perspective[44] we should further differentiate between risks and uncertainties.

The defining features of *risks* are that they can be quantified, have a specific statistical probability and are usually project-specific. Building a hospital in Switzerland involves a different level of risk than building the same

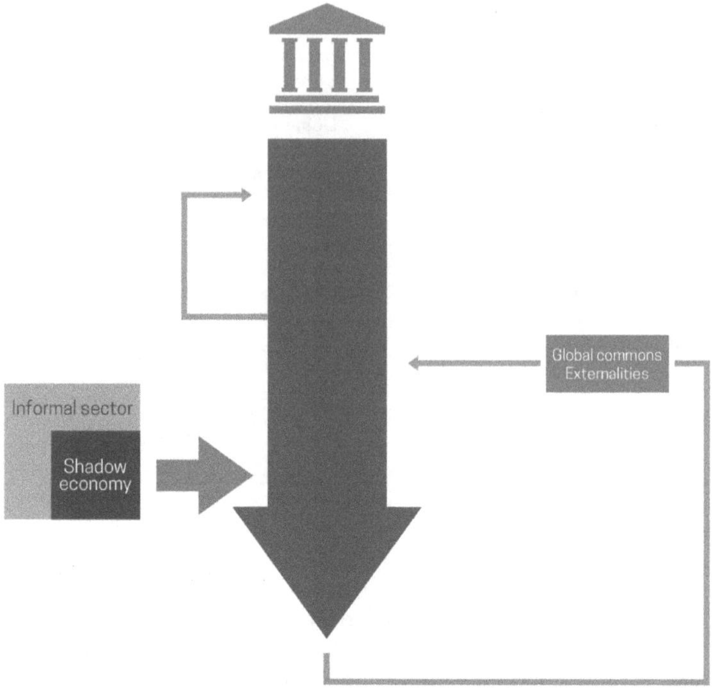

Figure 3.2 Traditional financing: end of pipe

hospital in a sub-Saharan country. We are able to put a price tag on the risk and can start trading and hedging it. Once we have identified a risk as a risk, we can try to avoid it or we can choose to either cover or relinquish the liabilities and responsibilities associated with it. However, we are not yet able to put an adequate price tag on physical risks affecting the real economy or the associated liabilities affecting the banking sector, nor on the risk of transitioning from a fossil-driven to a low-carbon system. The IMS is simply not holistic enough to provide a pathway to unlock the trillions of private-sector investments needed to generate revenue, absorb the systemic risks and fund and manage global commons. *Uncertainties*, meanwhile, are intrinsic to any complex system. They are not fully tradable, resist having any precise price tag applied and are not fully amenable to statistical analysis or probability measures. Uncertainties never disappear and require an entirely different kind of assessment.[45] Negative collective externalities include biodiversity loss, water stress, heatwaves, state failure, war or the sudden onset of mass forced migration.[46] If we have to live with increasing uncertainties, we may be forced to realise that we cannot wholly control or anticipate our future and will have to come up with prudent, failure-tolerant preventive measures that reduce the potential costs associated with them. Once we have identified and differentiated these different forms of the unknown, we can then decide how to manage them.[47] The more uncertainties we are confronted with, the more we need an altered mindset,[48] new technologies and an upgraded IMS to enable us to face these new realities. While predictive AI algorithms and big data correlations cannot eliminate unknown unknowns and uncertainties, they can help to transform unknown unknowns into uncertainties and some uncertainties into risks, though others will remain uncertain. This will allow us to put a price tag on identified risks so that we can hedge and trade them accordingly and find competitive private-market solutions for them. The reverse is true, too. The more uncertainties we are exposed to, the more we need different financial engineering tools to absorb, hedge, fund and manage them; this can be done by public or collective bodies in collaboration with the private sector. Such planetary uncertainties are manifold by their very nature. Some major elements affecting the IMS are summarised in Table 3.2.

Uncertainties never disappear but remain a constitutive element of any complex system and require an entirely different assessment. In short, underestimation and overconfidence need to be made a thing of the past, especially when it comes to the IMS, and we need a monetary mechanism that takes all the factors discussed above into account.

Uncertainty is a key characteristic of any complex system. Complexity refers to a state of affairs where the outcome remains undetermined and unpredictable by its very nature. Complex systems[49] are non-linear, meaning their outputs are not 100% determined and so are unpredictable.[50] Attempting to reduce complexity, for example, by increasing transparency, introducing a new taxonomy or simplifying processes through control, coercion or efficiency measures, is of little use. Even after such measures are taken, a system will remain complex and indeterminate. We cannot push the reset button on complex operations and start over, because everything will be different the second time round. While many social events and systems may be perceived as merely complicated,[51] they are first and foremost complex. They are multifactorial and do not allow for any simple cause–effect explanations

Table 3.2 General features of uncertainties affecting the IMS

Uncertainties affect us all in an asymmetric manner. Some people are hit harder than others.
They cannot be covered solely by private households, companies, commercial banks, private insurers, investors or individual states.
They are all interlinked, and cause tipping points, backlashes and overshoots in a non-linear way with fat-tail events.
They often manifest as force majeure (e.g. earthquakes, wars, state failures, social upheavals) in the short term and as multiple crises (e.g. global warming, biodiversity loss, serial pandemics, forced migration) in the long term.
They come on top of all the well-known general risks that each society has to cope with (unemployment, health crises, bankruptcies, economic downturns).

(causal chains). The intermediate results of any complex system therefore cannot be fully anticipated, as that system will have emergent properties. Applying this to the IMS and redesigning it accordingly means dealing with systemic uncertainties, which requires a completely different psychological and political strategy than that needed for complicated processes. We need to adapt and deal with our fear of uncertainty and incompleteness. And instead of trying to anticipate cyclical booms and busts using longitudinal historical data, we are confronted with a change in our societal state of being. It is rather like the different states of matter: solid, liquid or gaseous, depending on the circumstances. If we apply this metaphor to our current state of affairs, the task we are faced with is not to reinvent everything from scratch but rather to upgrade and rearrange what already exists in a different way. Figure 3.3 illustrates this general societal shift, for which the IMS is a key catalyst.

Phase 1 represents the well-known traditional boom-and-bust cycles. Transfer payments can help to navigate, balance and steer the economy. *Phase 2* represents the transition we are going through right now. It requires us to mobilise about eight to ten times more liquidity than usual. The entire process remains non-linear. *Phase 3* represents the new equilibrium we are heading for, once the transition is complete. Speaking in general terms, this equilibrium would reflect the recommendations of an ecological, regenerative, steady-state or circular economics, or an economics of well-being. During this transitional period, rather than generating clear-cut *1* or *3* states, we generate ones that are fuzzy, blurred and hybrid. This fuzziness or indistinctness will remain until we have completed the green transformation, integrated the new technologies and rebalanced our multipolar world. The IMS represents a powerful enabler and catalyst within a small window of opportunity while our biophysical reality (biodiversity, climate, water, soil, etc.) remains reasonably intact (Box 3.3).

Box 3.3 Biophysical reality – energy and the productivity function

One of the major reasons why economics in general and the monetary system in particular remain insensitive to biophysical reality is that academic economics has resisted the idea of a comprehensive marginal productivity function that includes energy.[52] Classical theories (Adam Smith, Ricardo, Marx) saw labour as the source of value, while neoclassical ones (Veblen, Jevons, Walras) also included land. The Cobb–Douglas marginal productivity function[53] assumed a coefficient of 0.3 for capital and 0.7 for labour, and Robert Solow[54] identified an unexplained residuum of 0.875. Energy (resources, land) did not play a crucial role. Over the last 150 years, we have tolerated an economics discipline that refuses to recognise energy as an independent factor.[55]

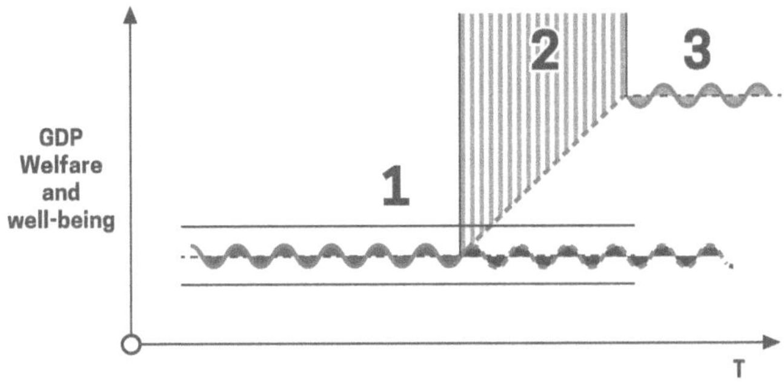

Figure 3.3 Altered states of societal organisation

If we wish to extend this idea to the financial sector, we should familiarise ourselves with synthetic asset-backed securities (ABSs), in which private equity and public entities play different but complementary roles; first-loss tranches; waterfall risk management; horizontal (tokenisation) and vertical (volume) scaling; diverse public–private partnerships (blended finance) for infrastructure projects[56]; unconventional currency swap lines between central banks and regulators, which make it possible to fund and hedge local risks of global hazards; central bank digital currencies (CBDCs) conditioned to provide upfront funding for international institutions (such as the WHO) so that they can tackle future pandemics, extreme weather and biodiversity loss; green quantitative easing (QE), which comprises upfront funding from MDBs and other development finance institutions (DFIs) that can be used to provide multiple hedging instruments (CDSs, public guarantees) for regional transition projects (public healthcare, education, etc.). The list is intentionally incomplete, in order to emphasise the (almost) unlimited possible permutations of financial engineering. And if we wish to extend this idea to the IMS, our goal should not be to adjust biophysical and political realities to the IMS, but the opposite: the scientific imperative and estimates of future costs should force us to see that the future needs to drive finance and not the other way round. The more successful we are at this task, the better (and cheaper) it will be for nature and humans alike. Beyond mere anti-cyclical spending, laissez faire capital and ad hoc adjustments, we should aim to reset the system itself. We are not yet close to the scale or speed we need to meet the challenges ahead. A new, upgraded, green IMS would not aspire to global governance but rather would be a *web without a weaver*, which would need suitable multilateral agreements to achieve universal prosperity. This is the Bretton Woods 2.0 moment, which I will discuss in later chapters.[57]

Between 1945 and 1971, the financial sector developed in parallel to the real economy, providing the liquidity and risk transformation needed to support the trade in goods and services. A shadow sector existed but had no systemic influence. The world was split into a more or less bipolar order. Technological innovation meant using a fax machine, a plane, a telephone or a TV. Ecological crises were seen as regrettable and inconvenient side effects of an economic growth process that was accepted overall; these effects were only ever local in scale. This all changed in the 1960s and 70s. Publications such as *Silent Spring* (1962)[58] and *The Limits to Growth*[59] provided an intellectual framework for rethinking the link between ecology and economics. The informal sector (fraud, illicit transactions and black-market activities) gained systemic relevance, while the financial sector, including securities, insurance, real estate and banking, gradually dissociated itself from the real economy over the decades.

In figures[60]: in 1980, the sum total of global financial assets (12 trillion USD) represented 120% of global GDP. That figure rose to 263% (56 trillion USD) by 1990, to 310% (119 trillion USD) by 2000, to 316% (219 trillion USD) by 2010 and 600% (500 trillion USD) by 2020. The mismatch has become particularly marked in the global currency market, where up to 98% of the 6,000 trillion USD of daily currency trading is speculative and only 2% involves real assets. The financial sector has been operating for decades without clear rules, creating its own revenue and disconnected from the real world. This has further increased the volatility of markets, and banking, currency and state crises have become the new normal. Even if we take human ingenuity to its maximum potential, there is no escaping the biosphere.[61] All economic activities are embedded in natural life, with all its scarcity and resource constraints, and we humans are an ineliminable part of it. It is not an exaggeration to characterise the current situation as one where we are operating in a quasi-non-system: footloose capital leading to unsurmountable externalities; atactic, ad hoc collaboration with unfair and brittle solutions; quick, ex post fix-and-repair measures that leave the underlying causes untouched; diffuse responsibilities and a lack of real benchmarking and taxonomies; massive spillovers and ill-defined liabilities. These add up to a monetary non-system, where we stumble from one crisis to the next, rather than having a monetary order in place that enables everyone to do business, follow their political agendas and lead their private lives.

One of the most significant symptoms of a monetary system that does not match with social, political and biophysical reality is its inherent instability, which results either from the inability to tackle and absorb real economic crises and stressors, such as systemic pandemics, harvest defaults or mass forced migration, or from dysfunctional design or a combination of the two. This mismatch is evident in a toxic mixture of massive trade imbalances, capital outflows, growing speculative bubbles (including real estate) and an unprecedented explosion of the monetary base (M0). Commercial credit expansion with increasing private and public debt ratios, all-time-high corporate profits and stagnating wages is another. Pro-cyclical, deregulated financial markets with low capital requirements,[62] complex, unregulated and opaque financial assets (Credit Default Swaps (CDS), Collateral Debt Obligations (CDOs), Asset Back Securities (ABSs)), an ever-growing shadow banking sector and a massive information asymmetry between those who create the financial products and those who buy them are signs that the current regime is under stress.[63] Between 1970 and 2010 alone, all these mismatches translated into at least 147 banking crises, 218 currency crises and 66 sovereign crises.[64] The overall output losses and costs include fiscal costs, real economic output losses, increasing public debts and non-performing loans reaching an average of 25% of GDP over a two- to three-year period.[65] In such a toxic environment, banking crises often precede currency crises. In some cases there was even a triple crisis: banking crisis, currency crisis and unsustainable debt crisis. More recent data shows there has been a further increase in instability ever since, with crises tending to last longer and be associated with a higher output loss.[66] Even if we will never be able to satisfactorily answer the 'chicken or egg' question – that is, to definitively say whether real economic activities caused the trouble or whether the financial sector did – we must acknowledge that the IMS is not acting as a neutral veil that simply reflects real economic activities.

In a multipolar, highly interconnected world, we are confronted with toxic pro-cyclical chain reactions, which deepen and prolong crisis after crisis and whose impacts are becoming more and more costly to repair. Having to constantly regulate, fix and repair a system signals that we cannot rely on its autopoetic, self-regulating power and that there might be something wrong with the design itself.[67] The proposals for an updated IMS that I explore in the next few chapters will not entirely eliminate all these financial crises, but a more stable and adjusted IMS could substantially contribute to financing our common future. Operating in a quasi-non-system, where ongoing crises cost on average 25% of GDP in affected countries, it seems to be irrational to continue business as usual, where we simply apply the existing rules and keep going as if there is no tomorrow. Instead, ad hoc and ex post political interventions[68] should be upgraded and adjusted through new rules and measures that more closely match reality. Imagining a more accurate monetary design that could reduce these costs by, say, a mere 25% would already represent a substantial indirect funding tool for a better future. And even if we don't agree with the notion and the momentum of a new international monetary order, but prefer business-as-usual scenarios, we must admit that the status quo has become extraordinarily expensive for all of us. In other words: *can we still afford the current IMS?*[69] Neglecting the new realities of systemic ecological crisis, a multipolar power game and new disruptive technologies will mean the current system is always behind the curve.

Our future should drive finance

While finance currently still drives opportunities and risks, it should actually be the other way round. We can call this a *zero-budget approach*. We should first establish a common agenda, taking account of all the unfulfilled opportunities and unchecked risks. That agenda should then drive finance to explore the most ambitious, innovative and advanced forms of financial engineering and monetary design possible so that both opportunities and risks can be addressed.[70] This approach is premised on the understanding that money is not a fact of nature and finance is not a natural law. Rather, it is one of the most important human inventions.[71] In this view, finance is a self-made operating system that we can use to either accelerate or destroy our common future. It can literally transform a bag of sand into a PhD, a hospital or a nursery, depending on how it is structured. Or it can transform that same bag into something destructive, like a tank or a landmine. In short, finance is a convention that can be used to benefit or harm humanity. And it's one that we have the power to change.[72]

Notes

1 This holds true for the Austrian and historical schools of economics, the physiocrats, Marxist and neoclassical theories, the traditional Keynesian approach, institutionalism and behavioural finance. None of them question the design of the monetary system itself or are able to describe the IMS and the associated risks as a complex system, and all of them use historical data to predict the future.

2 Interdisciplinarity in this context does not refer to the smallest common denominator, but to the specific contribution each discipline can make to a shared topic of concern. In the present context, finance and economics can make a specific contribution to determining the optimal allocation of means, the adequate liquidity to achieve a specific goal and adequate pricing under conditions of risk, uncertainty and scarcity. This is something no other academic discipline can yet do. In short, finance and the design of an IMS can make it possible to attain the 'cheapest of all worlds'.

3 See the World Academy of Art and Science's Tao of Finance working group and the Club of Rome's Finance Hub, which both apply systems-thinking approaches to finance and the IMS. See Brunnhuber 2020 and 2023 and, from the Club of Rome Finance Hub, Jess et al. 2023.

4 See German Marshall Plan 2024.

5 My own calculation, based on German GDP in 1991 and Böick and Lork 2019. See also Enenkel and Rösel 2022.

6 In general, we tend to hold on to a mindset, even if it is dysfunctional, until a better alternative is available. The seminal expression of this theory is Kuhn 1962. The tendency to cling to an outdated mindset is well documented not only in the literature on cognitive bias (as 'availability bias', which is related to 'confirmation bias', 'narrative bias' and the 'framing effect') but also to cognitive psychology in general as 'loss aversion'. However, in the present case we *do* have an alternative available to us: a systems-thinking approach. See Meadows 2008; Dörner 1996. With regard to economics, see Ormerod 2005; Buchanan 2013.

7 See Verbaanderd et al. 2021, Sattari et al. 2022 and Thelwall et al. 2023.

8 Larsen 2018.

9 See World Bank 2023.

10 If we compare VAT at 20%, compulsory social security at 25%, corporate income tax at 11%, personal income tax at 23% and property tax at 5% of overall tax intake, each taxation scheme has its own flaws. VAT-based tax intake for example requires a cash payback of up to 50% of the revenue to compensate for its regressive nature.

A progressive income tax risks people leaving the country. Wealth taxation is confronted with an endless list of corporate shares, which will ultimately increase unemployment and prices for consumers and drive down investment without offering a substantive alternative. See Saez and Zucman 2019; Piketty et al. 2023.

11 Sinn 2012.

12 Despite all these constraints, potential tax reforms should still include offshore and offsheet taxation, a global flat corporate tax and taxes on high-frequency trading and naked short selling. Those engaged in the last two types of trading will need to redefine their job description in the new era of the IMS. But the goal of these taxation schemes would be less to generate additional volume, and more to create a level playing field and steer the economy towards a greener future.

13 Deutz et al. 2020; OECD 2020.

14 UN Global Crisis Response Group 2023.

15 The loss and damage funds, for which 700 million USD has been pledged so far, are an example. With good intentions, we will end up with a 'too low, too slow' scenario. On top of that, the loss and damage funds rely on the functionality of the existing system that we are trying to overcome, which defeats the purpose.

16 Volz et al. 2020; Vasic-Lalovic et al. 2023; Zucker-Marques et al. 2023.

17 For further empirical data, see Schularick 2022.

18 This involves at least four aspects: (1) a legalistic versus an economic approach, any haircut would disadvantage concessional debt, indirectly subsidising other creditors (Lazard 2022); (2) a shift from collective action clauses (CACs), which require a hyper-majority to restructure loans, towards single-limb CACs, which allow restructuring throughout all bond series (Megliani 2021); (3) the harmonisation of soft debt relief measures, including interest rate reductions or maturities (Reinhart et al. 2016); and (4) adjusting the interest rate for SDRs to finance debt restructuring (see Paduano 2024).

19 External debt servicing as a share of exports has risen from 3.9 to 7.4% globally. Post-WWII agreements (such as the 1953 London Agreement) limited external debt servicing to 5% to avoid undermining domestic recovery.

20 The World Bank's HIPC Initiative, the G20's Multilateral Debt Relief Initiative, the Debt Service Suspension Initiative (DSSI) and the IMF's Catastrophe Containment and Relief Trust (CCRT) all share the common narrative that the debt burden remains an unmanageable vicious circle for poor countries, who find themselves caught on a treadmill with no end in sight.

21 Seery 2020; International Institute for Sustainable Development 2024.

22 The current commitment of the international community is 700 million USD, which equals about 0.2% of the damage. See The Guardian 2023.

23 For example, a 15% haircut would translate to a ten-year debt repayment period (Wang and Qian 2022). Each dollar provided by an MDB for debt relief would translate into 7 USD of additional fiscal space, which has higher leverage than additional lending (Zucker-Marques et al. 2023).

24 Tobin 1989.

25 The IMF's structural adjustment rules, which call for reduction of fiscal imbalances, privatisation of public goods, trade liberalisation and free capital flows, are also considered elements of austerity policy. See Williamson 1990.

26 Increasing public-sector finance will primarily involve more outcome-oriented measures and decentralised administration (see Alfonso et al. 2023). But even fully efficient administration would not be more robust and resilient to external shocks.

27 Soaring unemployment and additional negative spillovers to the healthcare sector (increase in morbidity and mortality) are the most prominent short-term effects. Loss of future productivity and competitiveness due to a lack of public investment in infrastructure (healthcare, education, energy, etc.) is a less obvious one that will leave society unprepared for future challenges. See Johnson 2017.

28 A system's resilience is enhanced by greater diversity and a higher number of pathways or greater connectivity because it will then have multiple channels of interaction to fall back on in times of crisis. However, these factors have the opposite effect on efficiency. Conversely, placing too much emphasis on efficiency sacrifices resilience: as streamlining increases, connectivity or diversity decreases. This sooner or later leads to systemic collapse. The opposite is true as well. If too much emphasis is put on resilience at the cost of efficiency, the system will not be viable either and will become stagnant. These points are of crucial relevance to the IMS, especially in the face of increasing banking, currency and debt crises. See Brunnhuber 2023 and Brunnhuber and Lietaer 2005.
29 See Taleb 2012.
30 The optimum point of the anti-fragile zone skews slightly towards resilience. This asymmetry demonstrates that resilience is more important to maintain a system's integrity than an emphasis on efficiency and austerity. This has important implications for how to redesign the IMS.
31 For an instructive phenomenology of how humans fail at complex decision-making, see Dörner 1996; see also Bazerman and Moore 2012. Our species did not evolve to deal with complexity, and so we are maladapted to the complexity of late modernity. On this topic, see the literature on 'evolutionary epistemology': Vollmer 1975 remains an insightful read, while Bradie and Harms 2020 presents some more recent research.
32 On this view, social and ecological spillovers, often associated with competitive market activities, are not market failures as such, but rather due to the lack of a properly configured market. If we had an IMS that struck a balance between efficiency and resilience, we would be better able to cope with ecological crises and ongoing externalities.
33 Force for Good 2024.
34 Semieniuk et al. 2022.
35 Aigner 2019; Damgaard et al. 2019.
36 See Galafassi 2023.
37 The same is true for mere behavioural changes at an individual level. As important as they are, they cannot provide the leverage necessary to shift our society in the necessary direction. Each time we give up something sinful (e.g., flying or eating meat), demand for the associated products will decrease and prices will fall for those who continue consuming them. In addition, isolated behavioural changes generate multiple rebound effects that further undermine the purpose of those changes. In order to be more effective, behavioural changes need to be embedded in an upgraded monetary framework, such as my proposal for a Bretton Woods 2.0. For further details on these behavioural biases see Brunnhuber 2023 and Sinn 2012.
38 75% of all climate finance circulates within Europe, the USA, East Asia and China. Emerging markets lack the finance to cover the impact of this global negative collective externality, as they face additional currency, project and political risks. The gap will be between 15 and 30 trillion USD by 2040. In order to cope with this flawed system of financial flows, we need an IMS that provides the liquidity necessary to overcome the constraints. See Climate Policy Initiative 2023.
39 Schroeder 2006.
40 According to Swiss Re and Climate Policy Initiative, catastrophic natural events and associated financial losses increased more than fourfold between 1970 and 2020. The estimated flow of global climate finance (one trillion USD in 2020) is less than a tenth of the 11 trillion USD required each year over the next 25 years to limit warming to 1.5°C. See Alberti 2024.
41 We should differentiate between commodifying and pricing our future on the one hand and the question of 'Who is going to fund, hedge and manage that price tag?'

on the other. The more we are confronted with collective externalities and global public common goods, the more the active state and an active regulator should lean in to fund and hedge the price tag. See Sukhdev 2012; Brunnhuber 2023.

42 The global carbon budget if we are to meet the 2°C target is about 40 billion tonnes, which would give countries an average of seven years to exit fossil energy completely. But we still have fossil resources available for decades: coal for 138 years, oil for 54 years and gas for 49 years. That means the vast majority of these resources have to stay in the ground and we have to come up with sensible financial mechanisms that respect private property and its expected revenue while also tackling the negative externalities associated with them. Instead of regulating the price, we could start limiting the volume (cap) and then start trading within these new biophysical boundaries. The relative price of goods and services would then adjust more efficiently than if we regulated the price in the first place. See Stavins 2022.

43 There is a vast body of literature on this topic, demonstrating over and over again that preventing damage is far cheaper than fixing it. One example is 'hysteresis': the restoration of an ecosystem once it has been destroyed. See Dasgupta 2021.

44 Markowitz 1959; Fama and MacBeth 1973.

45 The vast majority of events we may potentially face in the near future have the character of uncertainties rather than risks. Hedging, funding and managing these uncertainties will require a different strategy, emphasising (1) resilience measures over maximising efficiency throughputs; (2) preventive measures over managing damage; (3) collective and public endeavour over individual action; (4) modular and systemic thinking over linear and cause-and-effect processing; and (5) simple heuristic rules of thumb over the use of endless checklists, historical datasets and Excel spreadsheets as a way to pretend we can control uncertainties.

46 Applying the Lucas argument (Lucas 1976) that no economic intervention can be predicted using historical data from a period when the intervention did not yet exist, we should be careful in our assessment of future shocks. If we take the expected costs of climate change at 5% of global GDP, biodiversity loss at another 1.5 trillion USD and the costs of the last pandemic at over 15 trillion USD, we will get a sense of the magnitude of what we are facing.

47 This creates a vicious circle: inherent uncertainty in the financial sector translates into inherent instability in the political and corporate sector, which further translates into fear and irrational choices that can be measured in rises on volatility indexes in the stock, bond and currency markets. Major signs of this inherent uncertainty include the shadow banking system (worth over 200 trillion USD in 2024), the short-term repo market, soaring private debt, high-frequency trading and the multiple and fuzzy reuse of collaterals (rehypothecations). For further data see also Wullweber 2020.

48 One of the most promising approaches is the Inner Development Goals project, which emphasises the need to develop a mindset that goes beyond mere technological or rule fixes. See Inner Development Goals 2024.

49 Whereas reductionism tries to dissect, catalogue and analyse components to explain outcomes, complex systems are sensitive to the history of their own initial conditions. A dynamic characterised by open networking, multiple intermediary hierarchies, feedback loops and self-organising components will move beyond static equilibrium and lead to the emergence of new, unpredictable structures. See Šlaus 2020.

50 Bifurcations, attractors, critical thresholds and fractals with scale-independent isomorphisms shape and modify the ongoing process. Attempting to reduce complexity, for example by increasing transparency or by simplifying processes through control or coercion, is of little use. See Mandelbrot 1977; Mainzer 1997.

51 'Complicated' in contrast to 'complex' refers to a state of affairs where we have to learn, follow and apply a specific protocol in order to achieve a specific goal.

Manufacturing a watch, undergoing a neurosurgical procedure or flying a plane are complicated but achievable, rather than complex.

52 See Keen et al. 2019 and Keen forthcoming.

53 Cobb and Douglas 1928; Douglas 1976.

54 See Solow 1957.

55 More recently, biophysically informed economics has tried to factor in energy, and the entire picture of output, marginal productivity, aggregated GDP and price formation is starting to shift. According to these new theories, output is roughly equal to energy input minus the waste we produce in order to generate it. If we accordingly discount 'energy' from the productivity function, we can easily end up with negative net value added. See Ayers 2016 and Kümmel 2013.

56 This includes equity, credit lines, outcome bonds, multiple state guarantees, insurance schemes and mezzanine and hedging instruments. Currently, 1 USD of public money mobilises about 0.75 USD of private capital. The current blended finance regime clearly lacks the necessary speed and scalability, with the high hurdle rate of 8% for the private sector remaining a 'dry powder' to effectively mobilise private capital. For example, state guarantees are highly underutilised by MDBs, representing less than 2% of their portfolio with a call-in of 1:36. See Habbel et al. 2021; Attridge and Engen 2019.

57 See Georgieva 2020.

58 Carson 1962.

59 Meadows et al. 1972; Club of Rome (2022).

60 Dutta 2018. For figures for 2020, see Woetzel et al. 2021.

61 Dasgupta 2021.

62 The 'mark to market' rule, where assets are evaluated throughout the business cycle – with appreciations during boom and devaluations during bust phases – accelerates the pro-cyclical impact of the IMS. See Borio et al. 2001, Ellul et al. 2014 and – most notably – Shearer 2023.

63 The 1929 economic crisis led to the Glass–Steagall Act of 1933. Commercial and investment banks were strictly separated in order to prevent cross-subsidies and risk transfers that further destabilise the system.

64 Leaven and Valencia 2012.

65 Taking the most expensive events as a benchmark: fiscal costs as a proportion of GDP range from 30% (Korea 1997) to 57% (Indonesia 1997), debts from 60% (Nigeria 1993) to 100% (Congo 1992), output losses from 98% (Ecuador 1982) to 140% (Congo 1982). The data further reveals that in emerging economies the fiscal costs compared with overall financial system assets are twice as high as fiscal costs compared with GDP. This trend is reversed in developed countries, showing that a functional financial sector can play an important role in mitigating, adapting to and hedging future shocks. See Leaven and Valencia 2012; Schularick 2022.

66 Leaven and Valencia 2012; IMF 2023a; Brunnenmeier and Reis 2023.

67 This is 'Goodhart's law': whenever a regulation is implemented, there will be a creative innovation to bypass it that defeats the initial purpose. As Goodhart himself put it, 'Any observed statistical regularity will tend to collapse once pressure is placed upon it for control purposes' (Goodhart 1975), though the law is often stated more generally as 'When a measure becomes a target, it ceases to be a good measure' (Strathern 1997).

68 This traditionally included recapitalisation, nationalisation, liquidity support, state guarantees for bank deposits and an expansive monetary and fiscal policy. At the same time, the results of microprudential adjustments (risk diversification, bank restructuring, capital requirements, etc.) have been rather disappointing. Taking both measures – macro and micro – together, we should conclude that the policy interventions on one side acted as emergency aid, leaving the underlying incentives

untouched. One major difference from Bretton Woods 1.0, which introduced capital controls, is that any Bretton Woods 2.0 should link macroprudential interventions to the provision of conditioned liquidity assistance (COLA) to the market players in the financial sector. This would ensure stability and transformation at the same time. We will explore the relevance of COLA in subsequent chapters.

69 Because we are wired to have a strong short-term memory, we quickly forget the pain of a shock. The stock market plummeted by 26 trillion USD between July 2007 and November 2008, equivalent to almost 50% of total world GDP; the rescue package for the banking sector amounted to five trillion USD, and an additional stimulus package of two trillion USD was needed for the same crisis. A decade later, the COVID-19 pandemic caused an overall output loss of 13 trillion USD. This demonstrates that a system that is dissociated from the real world will cause self-induced collateral damage in that real world, incurring an intolerable cost (for the data see Sinn 2009, 86 ff).

70 In fact, we are neither always rational nor always irrational but rather search for mechanisms to adapt to a complex world. See Lo 2017.

71 Jacobs and Šlaus 2012.

72 Brunnhuber and Jacobs 2020; Jackson 2013.

4 Helping to set the course

Taxonomies, transparency and transition plans

For centuries, if not millennia, the course of people's lives was determined by 'Malthusian cycles'. Each time the population and birth rate increased, a decline in food supply, harvest defaults, wars or pandemics then set back the population growth and our well-being and prosperity. There was no real progress, and these cycles repeated themselves over and over again. But between around 1750 and 1820 the situation changed. With one exception, most of the ingredients for change had already been in place for centuries: by 1820, human societies had invented the wheel and printing press and learned how to make fire. We had nation states, a banking system and taxation in place. Mathematics, astronomy, religion, music and art as well as knowledge of human anatomy were already established. Copper, iron, wheat, meat, fruit, vegetables, bread and butter were available too. Most of the elements of daily life as we know it today were in place. Despite this, people's living conditions had not changed significantly for hundreds or even thousands of years. Human life remained the same from birth to death, and despite all these achievements the overall evolution of societies was determined solely by demographic factors. But around 1820, roughly 30 years – or just one generation – after the French and American revolutions, something astonishing happened that set in motion a whole new process unlike anything seen before in all of human history: the social empowerment of individuals to use their critical minds and creativity and engage in new forms of social cooperation. This human-centric mindset changed everything: universal suffrage, minority rights, nurseries and compulsory schooling, a ban on child labour, public health and hygiene measures, new corporate constitutions, freedom of trade, movement and establishment and the formation of a labour movement and trade unions fundamentally changed the playing field. And it was not in the first instance an increase in resource efficiency and capital accumulation that changed the course of history, but a fundamental shift in our mindset. It was in this era of Enlightenment, when human societies started to apply critical and rational thinking, that new forms of government, liberal democracies and rule of law began to emerge and modern science, education and technology took off. All these developments came prior to any capital accumulation

DOI: 10.4324/9781003499978-4

and resource allocation. In fact, it was this fundamental shift in our individual and collective consciousness that enabled us to think, perceive, act and behave differently, breaking the curse of the Malthusian cycles. A mere technological fix without a change in governance and mindset has never been a successful strategy in human history. It has always been the interplay between the two that enabled the cooperation, coordination and social inclusion necessary to shift our society towards greater wealth and health. Figure 4.1 illustrates this.

The current rise of and debate about a new taxonomy, the need for greater transparency about offsheet, offshore activities including black-market activities and the growing importance of new disruptive technologies and potential green transition plans were not part of the initial Bretton Woods agenda. But this time things are different. In the 2020s, these factors have all become relevant to a new, green and updated Bretton Woods 2.0. This chapter is therefore divided into the following sections:

- Taxonomies.
- Transparency.
- Transition plans.

Taxonomies, or how to put the toothpaste back in the tube

Across the globe, there are multiple taxonomies that provide new guidelines for investors, regulators and consumers. Each country puts a lot of regulatory effort into outlining and implementing these new standards. One of the most prominent examples is the European Sustainability Reporting Standards (ESRS), which define ESG (environmental, social and governance) standards for the EU.[1] The term ESG was formally introduced in 2004, but the associated activities go back to the early 1990s.[2] The general idea is to get companies and investors to consider specific sustainability standards in their investment decisions and adapt their strategies and balance sheets accordingly. Within a

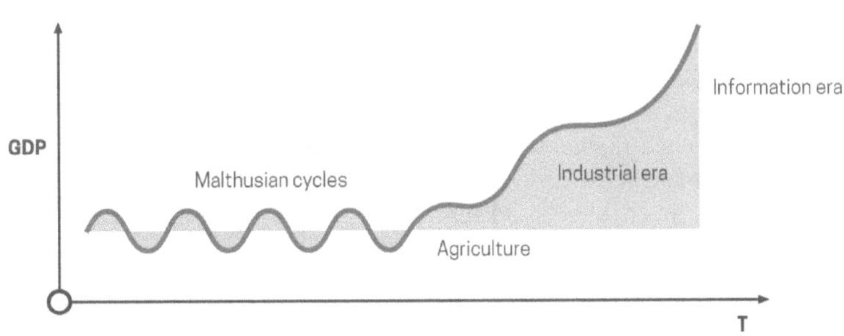

Figure 4.1 Malthusian cycles and the information age

competitive market, companies should be accountable for externalities and associated spillovers should be internalised on their balance sheets, thus helping to steer the entire economy towards a more sustainable future. At present (2025), about one-third of all assets under management globally take at least one of the three factors into account. In Europe, a minority of real economic investments consider climate issues as part of the environmental (E) component but neglect other environmental issues and do not consider social (S) and governance (G) dimensions at all. Over 700 metrics with dozens of categories can be observed, but there is little overlap between them, and greenhouse gas emissions do not appear to be an overarching common denominator.[3] Besides practical implications and limits, which represent a challenge in their own right, the general hostility to all ESG-related taxonomies is more conceptual in nature. Imagine you have three children. How do you decide which to favour over the others? Emile (E), Stefan (S) or Georgina (G)? Should military investments (tanks, munitions) be considered part of ESG, because they help to defend our free world? Would it be better or worse to invest in a fossil fuel company or one that produces landmines? Would it be better to push for a green transition at a polluting company's next executive board meeting or to exclude investment in that company from your portfolio? And, finally, who is accountable for all the associated negative externalities we are generating? The fuel extractors, the car industry, the drivers, the politicians or even the public transport system (trains and buses, for instance, often use petrol)? Or should we all be held accountable? And if so, what kind of regulatory frameworks and financial budgets are needed to address all the dilemmas? All previous taxonomies have been like a mixed salad bowl: full of appealing ingredients that don't go together. They are torn between inconsistent directives and attempt to insert more transparency into the system and further internalise and re-privatise externalities that we all generated collectively. It is commonly said that we can only manage what we can measure, but anything we can measure we can also manipulate, avoid and neglect.[4] It looks like, despite noble intentions, the entire ESG accounting system appears to produce a lot of noise but little value and no robust economic signals that would help steer our society towards a better future.

It is true that any ESG template expresses the non-financial risks of a company and represents a kind of shadow tax reflecting all the negative externalities associated with its economic activity. But factoring in all these costs on a corporate level is simply too expensive and/or too imprecise and the benefits too low to deal with the entire sustainability agenda. Instead of blaming the private sector, we should instead aim for an adjusted political agenda that sets new rules.[5]

Take Scope 3 directives,[6] which require companies to include and document all costs along their entire value chain. One example is the goal of banning child labour, where companies can make a real difference by ensuring children are sent to school. In doing so, they not only document a hazard but provide an incentive for change. The additional costs required to send a child to school, which is a collective and not a private responsibility, should come from additional liquidity assistance provided by the public sector. The same principle should be applied to ecological and governmental standards, too. In the next chapters, I will set out a proposal for an upgraded supply chain act to address this challenge. Under the current rules of the game, it is as if we are trying to put toothpaste back in the tube. An almost impossible and certainly very expensive endeavour. As a rule of thumb, investors do not invest in assets that don't correspond to their risk profile. Whereas specific project risks can be hedged, managed and internalised on the market, systemic risks cannot. Systemic risks are *negative collective externalities*, representing an overuse of global commons; they primarily follow biophysical laws rather than market rules. As long as we are unable to properly quantify such uncertainties, we will need a different, more integrated monetary system to cope with them. Financial disclosure directives are of little help to deal with the magnitude of all the crises ahead.

ESG standards reflect in a general sense any social, environmental and governance trade-offs we are collectively accountable for, and providing a new ESG-related taxonomy is definitely a powerful tool to address future problems. But it is not a stand-alone solution. We should instead advocate an *inventory approach*. The ESG standards allow us to better document our economic activities in the first place, put a price tag on unaccounted spillovers, adjust our balance sheets and redirect investor behaviour. Having no transparency about expenditures and therefore neglecting any inventorisation is not an option. That would make things even more expensive and uncontrollable, and just as random and unfair as ever, meaning the damage we have caused will not disappear and will remain unmanageable. Once we recognise the need for inventorisation, we will have to agree who is paying the bill. That means we will have to undergo the mental exercise of distinguishing between disclosure, documentation and billing. For the latter, we have two options. First, we could re-privatise the identified costs: that is, once the firms have documented and disclosed their activities, we legally oblige them to internalise those costs. However, we would then have to expect multiple leakages, avoidance strategies and exception policies, with increasing regulatory costs, greenwashing and bankruptcies. The time horizon left to exit the fossil industry is too short to rely solely on this policy measure. The entire process risks becoming atactic. The second strategy, once an inventory has been mapped out, is to designate all the damage we have caused as a negative collective externality that we are all accountable for. Dissecting the individual liabilities and reversing the entire engineering process will become an impossible task. So instead we will need to devise new hedging and funding instruments that involve (partial) interventions by international financial institutions.[7] The Bretton Woods 2.0 agenda seems a perfect candidate to achieve all this. In the next sections, I will make several proposals for how to overcome the constraints of the existing

ESG agendas. All this requires new rules, a new polity for the monetary sector and a more proactive role for international financial institutions.[8] Figure 4.2 illustrates the inventory approach.

1 represents the business-as-usual approach, which is the most expensive variant. *2* is the inventory approach, where we document and report losses and damage macro- and microprudentially. *3* is the current state of affairs, where we internalise and re-privatise negative collective externalities. *4* is the option of hedging and funding part of the ESG agenda through additional, conditioned liquidity assistance from the public sector. From a regulatory, policy and financial perspective, option *4* seems to be the fastest and cheapest way to address the trade-offs we are faced with. Public engagement is cheaper than re-privatisation and any upstream regulation is faster than downstream approaches.

Transparency, or shedding light and getting real

Besides formalised economic activities measured in terms of global GDP, any upgrade of the monetary system also has to factor in the relevance of the informal sector and black market, which are interlinked and contribute to the formal economic sector. Both already existed during the original Bretton Woods era but did not have the significance they do now. And both have always been a sign of a systemic deficit, since they grow in order to meet people's unmet needs. The informal sector consists of all non-regulated activities in our society, including home-based services and illegal activities involving drugs,

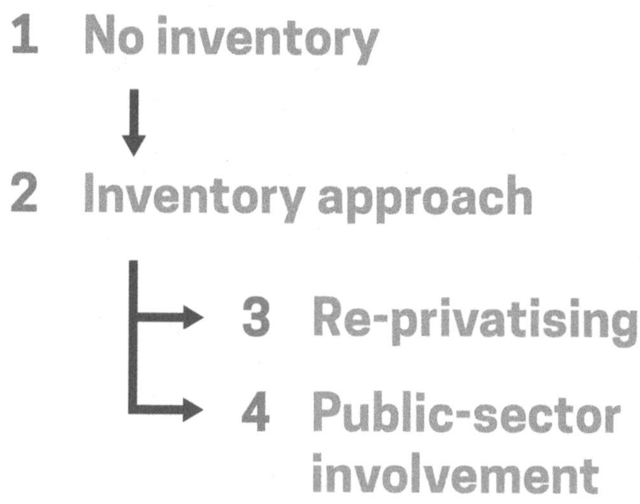

Figure 4.2 The inventory approach

human trafficking, money laundering and weapons. This sector is sometimes called 'system D', where D stands for the French *debroulliard* – meaning resourcefulness, the ability to achieve success in a complex, uncertain and unpredictable environment.[9] The main hallmarks of this system are that it is fully unregulated, untaxed and unmonitored; it is self-organising; it requires ad hoc decisions with no liabilities; and people working within it have no access to basic human rights such as social security, healthcare, trade union representation and paid holidays.[10] On a global scale, it accounts for up to ten trillion USD annually, employs approximately 1.8 billion people or up to 50% of the global labour force and mainly operates invisibly and in parallel to the official economy but without being accountable to it. Within the next decade, as hundreds of millions of young people reach working age, this ratio will most likely increase to two-thirds of the workforce, representing the second-largest economy in the world in relative terms. In this sense, System D is the largest field test of a fully liberalised, deregulated and singularised marketplace the world has ever seen.[11]

Besides the informal sector, there is also the black market and shadow economy, which comprises an ever-increasing financial dark pool and unregulated banking sector,[12] undocumented off-sheet and offshore activities and a vast number of illicit financial transactions, including fraud, corruption, money laundering, trafficking and the drugs trade. It accounts for at least one-third of our world GDP.[13] A widely used taxonomy for illicit financial transactions distinguishes between theft-type market activities, corruption, illicit tax transactions including mis-invoicing and the criminal market of human trafficking, drugs and weapons.[14] Empirical evidence attests to the magnitude of the problem. An increasing portion of private wealth, representing up to 10% of global GDP, is managed in unregulated tax havens, causing tax losses of over 200 billion USD every year. Terror financing amounts to almost three trillion USD and almost 10% of all global trade takes the form of illicit financial transactions. This results in a staggering global tax gap of over five trillion USD annually.[15] In this context, we are witnessing a corporate tax race to the bottom. Whereas rich OECD countries have been able to retain their general broad tax base, emerging and developing countries have lost it. From a purely administrative perspective, several hundred thousand additional tax officers are needed in Africa simply to meet OECD standards. All these informal and illegal transactions cement and exacerbate local inequality, reduce economic growth and social capital, further erode tax revenue, reinforce their own rules and pull our entire global economy in the wrong direction.

From a purely economic perspective, illicit financial flows (IFFs) have a different impact on the economy than other black-market activities. Any illicit inflows into a country generate income and jobs, but illicit outflows do not. The losses due to illicit outflows amounted to several trillion USD over the last decade, with a growth rate double that of formal domestic activities. In the Middle East, for every dollar of formal inflow from Offical Development Aid (ODA), foreign direct investment (FDI), remittance payments and philanthropy, an equivalent outflow of 2.8 USD in IFFs leaves the country undocumented. Mis-invoicing is the main cause. The general equation still holds that the volume of redirected ODA, military-related expenses, external debt payments and IFFs vastly outweighs the sum of official ODA, remittance payments and FDI. The monetary incentives in place make it next to impossible to generate sustainable domestic purchasing power at a level sufficient for a decent living. The case of ODA shows the dilemma especially clearly: of the 0.7% of world GDP dedicated to supporting the Global South, up to three-quarters is either indirect subsidies for prestige investments such as the military, is directed towards middle-income countries (where the money is less needed) or supports the donor country's domestic industry. Only a quarter is 'real' ODA.

For decades, we have been trying without success to readjust, prosecute and harmonise regulatory efforts to formalise and legalise the illicit sector. But these efforts are like the curse of Sisyphus: if we were suddenly to abolish this complex basket of activities, the world economy would collapse immediately. The informal sector thus acts as an important stabiliser, interconnected with the formal, conventional financial and real economy, yet pulling our entire society in the wrong direction. Instead of shutting it down, we would be better advised to look for mechanisms that incentivise all actors to behave in ways conducive to a better future. And instead of focusing all diplomatic and political efforts on re-regulating and consolidating the existing system, an upgraded International Monetary System (IMS) should change the rules of the game and gradually formalise the informal sector by slowly but surely pulling trade and commerce out of this basket and redirecting them towards a green and sustainable future without disrupting the overall built-in economic capacity and at the same time systemically drying out illicit transactions. An upgraded IMS that makes the informal sector less attractive and provides opportunities to live in a green marketplace will therefore need to be a substantial aspect of any future endeavour. New technologies, in particular Artificial Intelligence (AI) and blockchains, can play a crucial role in shedding more light in the dark, getting real on social human rights and providing more transparency for all (Box 4.1).

Box 4.1 New technologies facing new realities

Unlike in the Bretton Woods 1.0 era, when technology did not play a critical role, in the 21st century, we need new technologies to manage the increasing complexity we are faced with. It is similar to the shift from the agricultural to the industrial era when the emergence of new technologies (such as the steam engine and the lightbulb) was accompanied by a new political framework: the liberal order. In the information age, general-purpose technologies not only operate cross-sectionally but add another layer of complexity, crossing and blurring the natural boundaries between biological, physical and societal realities. Brain–chip interfaces will transcend the boundaries between physiological processes and technology in a way that a hammer, wheel or steam engine could never achieve. Or consider how the advances of the Internet of Things (IoTs) are becoming a global digital neural network, with sensors providing real-time information on the state of the earth and helping us to react appropriately.[16] AI, big data analytics, quantum computing, robotics, the IoT, drones, smart grids, renewables, energy storage, next-generation nuclear, e-mobility, blockchains, 3D printing, nanotechnology and materials science, gene editing[17] – most of these things cut across the private and public sectors and the dualism of science and humanities,[18] and have become a critical element of the transformation process and the IMS that is orchestrating it. Technology has become one of the major building blocks for change. What is missing is the polity and the adequate funding to make it happen.

Green transition plans, or how to enable the change

The transition will not come for free and it will affect all countries, irrespective of their political agenda. To finance the official UN Sustainability Development Goals (UN SDGs), for example, OECD countries will need about 2–4% of their GDP, and for the Global South that figure doubles to 4–8%. In the EU, there is a 40-trillion-euro funding gap for the transition to a low-carbon economy by 2050.[19] 30 trillion of that total comprises replacements and reallocation of investments and about ten trillion is additional investments. These additional investments are equal to about 2.3% of the EU's GDP, or around 50% of the cost of imported fossil energy. That will require a doubling of public spending from 250 to 510 billion euros per year to unlock private investments and fund public goods equalling 1.6% of the EU's GDP.[20] Three aspects are worthy of particular note here. First, additional fiscal tools to help businesses deal with significant depreciation on property, plant and equipment, exemptions from capital gains tax and a loss carry-forward for all asset classes, in order to drive the transition in the private sector. Second, new financial tools will play a role in mobilising additional private capital to hedge these additional investments. Third, additional liquidity is needed to fund and manage our planetary commons.[21] But this is just half of the story. Transitioning towards a greener and stabler future requires us to admit that we are facing a dual cost curve: the costs of adaptation and mitigation, as discussed above, simply represent an investment in a better future. Whereas mitigation measures are more likely to be incentivised through the private sector, adaptation measures require proactive public-sector activities. Such investments create jobs, generate revenue and provide opportunities. The second category of costs relates to managing the transition itself: disaster management, political instability, additional healthcare costs, welfare losses, food and energy price inflation, harvest defaults and financial losses due to stranded assets. This second cost component is orders of magnitude greater than the first. The dynamic between the two is simple and striking. Both costs add up in the first phase of the transition. The longer we wait, the higher the overall costs will be. Having the adaptation and mitigation costs properly funded and managed as soon as possible will mean that the costs of managing multiple disasters will decrease over time. That seems obvious from a clearsighted look at the facts, but actually taking the required action is hard. Again, the structure of the IMS is key. From a financial perspective, we can say that *hedging systemic risks, mobilising private capital, buffering unforeseen uncertainties, funding global commons and conditioning all these financial activities will translate into sustainability.*

The calculation for the EU given above only includes climate-related issues. If we adjust this figure to reflect the total costs of restoring nature reserves and repairing our adverse impacts on ecosystems[22] as well as non-sustainability-related costs such as preventing future pandemics (which requires massive upfront funding for the WHO and the public healthcare sector) and infrastructure spending (police, law enforcement, public administration, tax officers, sewage and waste management), I would tentatively suggest adding another two to three trillion USD to the total, bringing us to an additional 10% of global GDP. This can help us get a sense of the magnitude of what we are facing. To make this large number more manageable, it needs to be broken down into smaller chunks. That can be done by asking a series of questions. First, how are we to fund and manage planetary commons (like the Amazon rainforest) and domestic and local commons (healthcare, public infrastructure)? Second, how are we to mobilise and hedge private capital? Third, how are we to fund, enable and scale up new technologies so as to further increase efficiency and achieve the first two targets? When devising a green transition plan, we should be carefully evaluating existing financial tools that need simple adjustments, while also developing new forms of financial engineering to address new challenges.

The aim of any financial transition plan is to provide the regulatory framework, liquidity, financial assets and resources necessary to achieve certain targets as efficiently and effectively as possible. The targets themselves are generally set by political and societal consensus. The UN SDGs are examples of such targets. Achieving them will require additional trillions of dollars of liquidity and financial assets each year for the next ten to fifteen years. Additional, conditioned liquidity could help to provide these trillions. The greater the systemic risks, the greater the role for public bodies and a public monetary aggregate. Moreover, financial transition plans require us to look at the entire process along a timeline and to prioritise the funding accordingly.[23] If we distinguish between immediate support and remedies, medium-term changes and more systemic and institutional reforms,[24] most if not all targets will require an upfront loading of some sort of additional liquidity. The flowchart (Figure 4.3) provides a first model for the transition with some preliminary examples, which are explained in more detail later in this book .

Mobilising private capital

Private capital is crucial for the transition. But the very nature of private capital is that it is pro-cyclical, short-termist and risk-averse. The regulated international capital market comprises the stock and pension markets, with a value of about 110 trillion USD. This money has already been spent and invested but needs to be substantially redirected. On the other side, global net savings,[25] factoring in all cash deposits and saving accounts, amount to over 30 trillion USD. Whether we unlock and redirect private capital from the international capital market in a top-down way or mobilise a certain portion of domestic savings[26] from the bottom up, we will require additional financial instruments to hedge and manage multiple systemic risks, including currency risks and risks of civil war, corruption, legal prosecution and expropriation, as well as changes in domestic tax schemes to protect these private capital flows. However, the devil is in the detail. The cost of capital represents the return for the investor to compensate for an alternative asset or a perceived loss. The relative cost of capital to invest in a renewable energy site, for example, is determined by two classes of risks, which both add up. Macro or systemic risks (political, currency) are leveraged on a country level and micro or project risks (construction, defaults, domestic regulation) are hedged and managed on the spot. While the micro risks are equal or even lower in most BRICS+ states when compared with the G7, the macro risks are two to three times higher in developing countries, reflecting the significantly lower cost for G7 governments to borrow money.[27] In fact, most money (84%) flows uphill to OECD countries at low rates and then re-enters the Global South with a

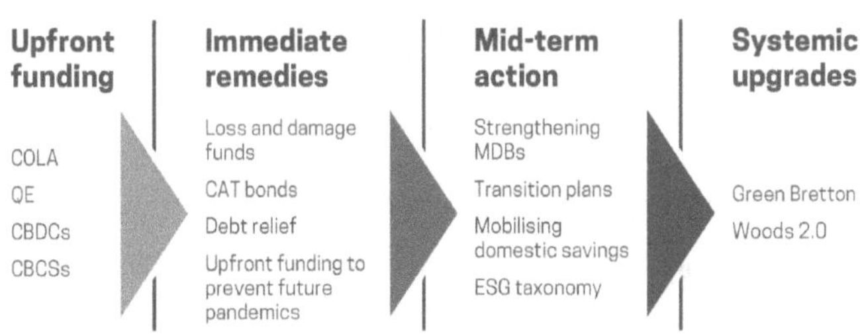

Figure 4.3 The timeline for transition

COLA: conditioned liquidity assistance; QE: quantitative easing; CBDCs: central bank digital currencies; CBCSs: central bank currency swaps; IFIs: international financial institutions

Table 4.1 Outline of a green transition plan

A		
	Prioritisation	Decisions based on ROI, KPIs and empirical evidence
	Taxonomy	Multiple disclosure directives
	Regulation	Shadow economy and informal sector
	Technology	Predictive AI, big data, blockchains
	Reform	Voting quota, investor dispute settlement, rating agencies, supply chain act, clearing house for derivatives
	CBCSs	Conditioned currency converter for LICs and MICs to tackle imported inflation and finance the UN SDGs
	COLA	Conditioned liquidity assistance for the private and public sector
	Green QE	Zero-coupon perpetual facilities, preventing bank runs, non-defaultable loans (NDLs), operates like a monetary anchor
B		
	Regulation	Enforced depreciations on property, plant and equipment, capital gains tax exceptions, loss of carry-forwards for all asset classes
	Philanthropy	Donor-driven grants, loans or bonds, often conditional, crowding-out effects
	Taxation and subsidies	VAT, earmarked sin/corporation/wealth/ international tax, offshore sites, expanded tax base, tax spending
	Private equity	Impact funding, venture capital, start-up co-financing, short-term, risk-averse
	Domestic savings	Mobilising domestic savings accounts
	Hedging risks	Credit spread, longevity swaps, foreign currency derivatives, inflation swaps, asset class risk stratification, CDSs, interest rate
	Credit lines	On-balance-sheet (bank loans), off-balance-sheet (special-purpose vehicles), MBSs (mortgage-backed securities)
C		
	Debt restructuring	Haircut, adjusted maturity and interest rate, debt-to-X swaps
	Blended finance	Asset-backed securities (ABSs), advance commitment strategies (ACSs), public endogenous credit creation (PECC), public–private equity shares (PPESs)
	Special drawing rights	Providing additional liquidity to fund/hedge and manage public goods, access for lower and middle-income countries (LICs, MICs)

high hurdle rate and additional costs, causing a net drain of over 15 trillion USD between 2004 and 2023.[28]

Mobilising private capital to invest in renewables in the Global South therefore requires a public and collective effort to pool and hedge these systemic risks. In the next chapters, we will see how regulators and central banks could provide an additional, conditioned monetary facility for a counter-cyclical mandate of the IMF and MDBs to (partly) guarantee, fund, hedge and manage this delta.

And again, the longer we wait, the more expensive it will be. If we miss this window of opportunity during which our ecosystem is still reasonably intact and nation-states are still functional, we will eventually lose the capacity and leverage of the IMS to steer us into a better future. That is why transition plans are a vital element of any Bretton Woods 2.0 agenda. Any lost opportunity will ultimately affect everybody. Whether we are poor with no assets at all, have negative savings, run a business, have a bank account, are institutional investors or enjoy the benefits of being a billionaire or a well-off pensioner, each of us has skin in the game and should agree to adjust the rules of that game. Any additional investment will be beneficial for all of us, as we are reducing the costs for future social and ecological externalities (unemployment, adaptation and mitigation costs) and providing opportunities for future generations (education, healthcare and infrastructure). Table 4.1 provides a preliminary list of principles for a green financial transition plan.

Notes

1 The ESRS are published by the European Financial Reporting Advisory Group. See EFRAG 2024.

2 See Pollman 2022. There are significant similarities to the introduction of new macroprudential metrics and measures in parallel to GDP, including the Human Development Index (HDI), the Genuine Progress Indicator (GPI) (see Kubiszewski et al. 2013), the Thriving Places Index (TPI) (see Centre for Thriving Places 2024) and Wealth Accounting and the Valuation of Ecosystem Services (WAVES) (see World Bank 2021). They all share a recognition that our current measures of prosperity and well-being do not adequately consider negative impacts on our ecosystem.

3 For example, ESG templates in Africa do not necessarily match those used in Europe, Asia or the US. See Barman 2018 and Cort and Esty 2020; for an analysis of the different stages of ESG disclosures, see Singhania, Monica; Saini, Neha (2022).

4 The inter-rater reliability is over 99% in the conventional credit ranking but drops to less than 50% for ESG templates, which makes the entire process largely invalid. In addition, the difference between a causal effect and mere correlation has not been clarified statistically: do ESG standards make a firm more successful or is it that only firms that are already performing strongly are able to adopt ESG standards? ESG funds in general require higher management fees (more than 50% higher on average), which translate into higher regulatory efforts and costs. See Berg et al. 2022.

5 To get a little more technical: the Sustainable Finance Disclosures Regulation (SFDR) offers a preliminary framework in Article 6 (mainstream), Article 8 (support

for ESG) and Article 9 (active investment in ESG with specifically tailored key performance indicators (KPIs). About 50% of all funds comply with SFDR Articles 8 and 9, but only 3% of all investments comply with Article 9 and over two-thirds of funds in this category do not have any specific ESG criteria. At present (2024), the entire disclosure process is a statistical artefact with little to no real economic impact. In addition, Article 2 (17) SFDR only refers to disclosures of corporate activities but does not impose any obligation to become green. In order to simplify this inefficient and opaque process, we should require investors to comply with Article 2 (17), add DNSH (do no significant harm) and PAIs (principles of adverse impact) and then forget the rest. This would also significantly increase comparability with other ESG templates.

6 See CDP 2023.

7 To be more precise: investors first apply Article 2 (17) SFDR (as explained above) and are then encouraged to invest in G-funds (which focus on (mis)management of human rights issues), E-funds (which provide expertise on climate change and nature reserves) and S-funds (which focus on human capital and basic social needs). Finally, the public sector steps in with state guarantees and hedging instruments to complement the rest of the ESG template. Readers might not fully agree with this approach politically, but it is the cheapest way to finance our transition. On the current debate, see also Finance Watch 2024.

8 The objection is that we will face moral hazards and free-rider effects. However, on this proposal moral hazard is substantially reduced as the investor is committed to at least one of the three ESG components and the complementary commitment of the public sector is conditioned. I will discuss the significant role of this kind of conditioned liquidity assistance (COLA) in the next chapters.

9 See Neuwirth 2012.

10 Looking at the informal sector through the lens of property rights, it probably represents one of the largest sleeping giants in the world economy. The Peruvian economist Hernando de Soto estimated the total value of undocumented and untitled property rights to be over 13 trillion USD. This represents over 50 times more than any ODA or FDI in less developed countries. In fact, only about one-third of the world's population has access to property rights and only up to 10% of African land is registered and formally documented; 90% remains *terra nullius*. This has a severe negative impact on any regional wealth creation. Up to three billion people globally live on communal, unregistered land, and over one billion live in fear of being evicted from that land because of lack of clarity about who owns it. Done the right way, land titling can substantially increase the productivity of agricultural activities and create the preconditions for a decent life. Only clear, legally bounded property rights entitle people to trade, subdivide, collateralise, sell and buy land titles, allowing the poor to participate in the world economy and generate wealth independently and on the spot. Accordingly, we need much more capital, not less, but it needs to be distributed differently and we need to address the vast majority of the world population that lives on untitled land. See Soto 2001 and 2015.

11 Studies have found that societies with a large informal sector are more resilient to financial crises, suggesting that this sector may act like an anti-cyclical buffer in the event of a shock. From a systems perspective, the informal sector serves an inclusive, anti-cyclical and reparative function in conventional economies that have one market and one monetary system to allocate goods and services. Any time this monopoly becomes unstable, there is a shift towards the second, parallel system that is not subject to the same conditions.

12 Investors and firms provide bank-like services through special-purpose vehicles and systematic investment plans, which are unregulated and informal. On non-bank financial institutions, see also Pozsar et al. 2013; Adrian and Ashcraft 2016; Adrian and Jones 2018.
13 Black-market activities only amount to one-third of all global financial activities. See Shaxson 2018.
14 Black-market activities are endemic and systemic, especially in the public sector. According to Transparency International (2022), the average corruption index globally is 43 out of 100. We therefore need mechanisms in place that reduce rather than reinforce these sectoral activities. I address this issue in the following chapters.
15 If we crunch the data further, we can see that over 20% of the tax gap is due to transnational corporations and 80% due to individual businesses and SMEs, which mainly trade informally and in cash. Corruption costs the world community 2.6 trillion USD and money laundering up to 1.6 trillion USD. The global revenue losses due to tax base erosion and profit shifting have risen to over 250 billion USD annually. These figures demonstrate the magnitude of the amounts lost to the public sector. It appears next to impossible to regulate such volumes within the existing monetary system. See Cobham and Janský 2018.
16 See Peng et al. 2020 and Greengard 2021.
17 Almost 50% of future success in implementing the UN SDGs will depend on these new technologies. Similar to previous developments in the industrial era, these new technologies can increase productivity by 1.5% per annum and scale up our GDP by over 25%. See Force for Good 2024.
18 Brunnhuber 2024.
19 For most OECD countries, the ratio between additional/new investments and replacement investments is 2:3. Take Germany: the country needs about two trillion euros over 20 years in new and additional investments and about three trillion euros in replacement investments. In the Global South, this ratio is far more skewed towards new investments, ranging between 5:1 and 10:1. In any case, we need much more liquidity in the global market rather than less. See Songwe et al. 2022.
20 See Institut Rosseau 2024.
21 Rockström et al. 2024.
22 There are several approaches to calculating the costs of ecological restoration and conservation. I am using the 'avoidance cost approach'; see Bainbridge 2023.
23 If we start prioritising the UN Agenda for Sustainable Development, using an ROI analysis and taking less spectacular but highly efficient and highly preventive measures, we can do more good than by simply providing the 175 billion USD in ODA per year. Such measures include investing in education (ROI 1:30), maternity and postnatal health (ROI 1:87), anti-malaria campaigns (ROI 1:48), improved nutrition (ROI 1:33), child vaccination (ROI 1:48) and skilled migration (ROI 1:20); stimulating trade and specialisation (ROI 1:7 for OECD countries and 1:99 for LDCs); and introducing a sin tax on nicotine, sugar and/or alcohol (ROI 1:23). Prioritising projects according to this list could save 4.2 million lives per year and an investment of 35 billion USD/year would have a social benefit of 1.7 trillion USD. See Lomborg 2023.
24 See Prime Minister of Barbados 2023 on the Bridgetown 2.0 Initiative.
25 See Global Economy 2024.
26 The global savings rate amounts to 23–28% of GDP. China holds about 8.2 trillion USD equivalent, India, Russia and Germany about one trillion, Africa about 400 billion. Most of these savings are located in domestic cash deposits in the Global North. One way to mobilise this money would be a green citizens' cash deposit,

where the state provides a higher interest rate and a public guarantee with a tax-gain exemption over the entire maturity.

27 Persaud 2023.

28 This contradicts neoclassical theory, according to which factor mobility between capital and labour should set a new global equilibrium. See Kindleberger 1987 and Lucas 1990. In reality, however, imperfect contractions, illicit transactions, political instability, inflationary pressure and being forced to hold high foreign exchange reserves collectively prevent the Global South from building up the required capital to overcome this toxic, unhealthy and expensive cycle (Buchner et al. 2023). Joint capital market programmes (J-caps) are better suited to mobilising domestic savings for domestic bonds (Volz et al. 2024).

5 Resetting the framework

The new game in town

I define regulators as the institutions and public agencies that get to set the rules of the game in the monetary sphere. That includes (with some overlapping responsibilities) central banks, the Bank for International Settlements, treasuries and international financial institutions such as the World Bank, the International Monetary Fund (IMF), the World Trade Organization (WTO) and Multilateral Development Banks (MDBs). These public bodies have a political mandate to make relevant decisions upstream and to allow other (international) public entities, such as the WHO, and private actors, such as institutional investors, large transnational companies and hedge funds, to act accordingly downstream. 'Setting the rules of the game' relates to polity measures, while all other actors pursue policies and practices within the framework of these rules.[1] This distinction is crucial to better understand the design of a new and upgraded Bretton Woods 2.0. Instead of taking an ideal-typical, academic greenfield approach (which will never succeed) or advocating ad hoc, business-as-usual procedures where we muddle through with a monetary non-system (which will be too expensive), we should instead support a practical intermediary step that takes account of the existing institutions but dares to transcend and upgrade their potential in terms of speed and scale, providing new financial engineering tools and clarifying some fundamental structural features of any monetary system in order to meet present and future requirements. In general, we would be better advised to adopt a systems-thinking mindset, which tries to integrate interdisciplinary findings from other disciplines, rather than one specific school of economic thought. The approach to monetary governance that regulators should consider is grouped around four fundamental principles:

- Money is not neutral.
- Triangulation is key.
- The potential of Central Bank Digital Currencies (CBDC) and its swabs lines must be harnessed.
- We need to transition to a green monetary ecosystem.

DOI: 10.4324/9781003499978-5

Money is not neutral

Our financial market is one of the few international institutions (and perhaps the only one) in which most, if not all, actors are embedded. Despite their different political agendas, every country – whether it be a Western-style democracy or an autocracy, a developing economy or a failed state – operates within the existing monetary system. Neither international religious institutions like the Catholic Church nor globally active NGOs like the WWF, the Red Cross, the Club of Rome and the World Academy of Art and Science have the reach or acceptance that the IMS has. Even terrorist organisations, the black market, criminal activities (fraud, illicit transactions, corruption) and the informal sector depend in some way or another on a functional global financial market. In this general sense, the international global capital market, its associated institutions (IMF, World Bank, central banks) and its monetary policies determine the rules of the game for fiscal policy, real economic activities, investor decisions, non-profit commitments and household spending. The IMS acts like an attractor for the good and the bad. For as long as we overlook the crucial role of the monetary system, we will fail to understand its relevance and potential integrating function. Instead, we all act like a fish in water, swimming around without thinking about our environment. We take the IMS as a natural law and respond accordingly. But we could instead step out of the water and critically question our assumptions. The traditional view excludes money from the equation that can be represented as a triangle between the real economy, the social world and the environment. This view looks at sustainability from three different angles and comes up with the smallest common denominator, which entirely overlooks the relevance of the IMS and so paints a misleading picture, since the monetary system has always been there, acting like an attractor or a funnel at the core of our society. Figure 5.1 illustrates this.

This blind spot prevents us from looking at the entire process from a systemic perspective. The IMS is the elephant in the room that nobody talks about. Money is not a thing or a natural law, but rather a convention, a social mechanism, a club rule and a set of legal codes that we can change as we see fit. Its current architecture runs counter to the goal of a sustainable future and prevents us from integrating the market system of the real economy and

Figure 5.1 The monetary system serves as an attractor and integrator

Table 5.1 Money is not neutral – six elements of the current system that are damaging our future

Pro-cyclical amplification of boom-and-bust cycles	Banks provide and withhold credit lines according to the requirements of the real economy and amplify the cycles instead of counteracting them.
Short-term perspective and aversion to risk	A discounted cash flow enforces short-term decision-making and avoids risks rather than hedging them.
Compulsory growth	A compound interest rate forces states, companies and households to grow to pay back their debts.
Destruction of social capital	Instead of encouraging trust, solidarity and cooperation, fear, greed and parasitic competitiveness are enforced.
Widening income/wealth inequalities	Current incentives support financial assets rather than real economic needs, further increasing the income and wealth gap.
Multiple rebounds	Efficiency gains are cancelled out by increased consumption that further hinders progress towards a sustainable pathway.

its systemic social and ecological externalities. Moreover, the current IMS chronically underfunds our global commons, mismatches systemic risks and uncertainties and overlooks the pro-cyclical and short-term dynamics of the financial market. There are at least six core elements to the current monetary system, which are outlined in Table 5.1.

If we had an upgraded monetary system that first respects the achievements of the existing financial architecture but remedies its flaws and constraints, we might have a powerful tool to integrate a dissociated financial market and create a healthier and wealthier planet. *Traditionally*, we mainly redistribute money from the private sector in order to fund, manage and hedge public goods and global commons.[2] However, this 'end-of-pipe' approach is slow, small in scale, administratively demanding and insufficiently targeted to meet the challenges we face in the Anthropocene era. Any time we produce a good or provide a service, we are contributing to biodiversity loss, climate change and land degradation, which in turn incur additional costs as we must manage the resulting damage. We create multiple negative collective social and ecological externalities that will eventually feed back. And 80% of the value chain is still dependent on fossil energy. At the same time, the entire economy is affected by the shadow economy and informal sector, which pull all economic activities in the wrong direction. The standard approach is to first generate social and ecological externalities, then create a compensation mechanism and finally fund global commons. Assuming a 3% global growth rate, the total annual conversion rate from fossil to green energy would need to be at least 5% to override the existing growth dynamic within a timeframe of 20 years. This means that 5% of the entire global value chain, including all income, profits and revenue, would need to switch to a non-fossil energy source every year. Because each time we build a solar panel or buy an electric car, we still generate income and revenue that are up to 80% dependent on fossil energy. This is one major reason why we need to upgrade the currency system itself to incentivise and consolidate green investments and generate multiple positive second-round effects that drive transformation towards a sustainable future. The next three sections will explore these requirements.[3]

Triangulation is key

Instead of advocating a specific school of economic thought, systems thinking can provide an out-of-the-box solution to generate the funds needed to finance global common goods *and* to de-risk and mobilise trillions of private-sector liquidity at the same time. We are traditionally caught between polarities like state and market, economy and environment, and private and public sector. But instead of looking for the smallest common denominator between these polarities while still maintaining their dichotomy, we should start recognising the differences between the two poles, acknowledge their limitations and transcend them by introducing a third party, namely, the regulators and central banks. In the traditional view, central banks and regulators remain passive, indirect and reactive, and competitive markets and state interventions are seen as antagonistic rather than complementary to each other. In order to overcome this silo approach, central banks need to become proactive and preventive, orchestrating and facilitating private-market activities and state interventions at the same time. This kind of monetary triangulation can become a forceful integrator, enabling us to face collective externalities and common goods together. It would allow us to shift towards a Pareto-superior equilibrium so that we end up with more, not less, competitive markets and a stronger, more resilient public sector.[4] The current situation resembles a Nash equilibrium, where, given a certain set of rules, two opposing agents have reached a position where they are no longer willing to further collaborate without harming their own position. Our Nash equilibrium is global in scale: North versus South, state versus market, economy versus environment and private versus public. The only way to transcend these multiple lock-in effects is to introduce a third party, accepted by both sides, that approves new rules ensuring the best possible outcome for all involved. Regulators and central banks could play that role. Figure 5.2 illustrates this.

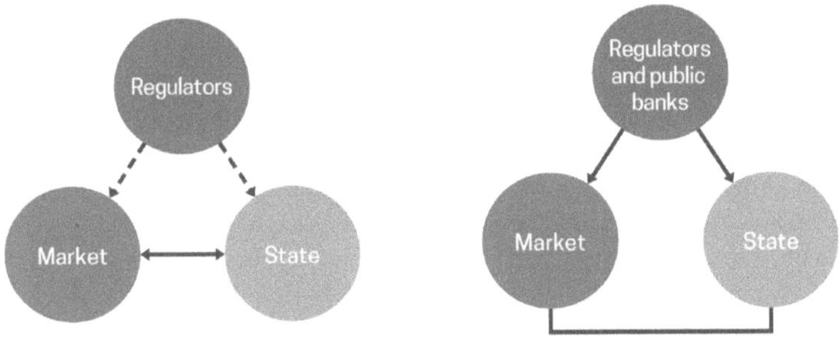

Figure 5.2 Overcoming polarities – triangulating the system

The potential of Central Bank Digital Currencies (CBDC) and its swabs lines must be harnessed

At present, over 110 out of 131 countries are developing, using or experimenting with CBDCs.[5] The design is clear, but the full scope of their relevance and impact is not. The idea is that central banks will create a new form of money. From a historical perspective, this new monetary aggregate is the fifth step in a process that started with coins (1), later followed by paper bills (2), the monopoly of national central bank money (3) and the fractional reserves of the commercial banking system (4). Each step enlarged the monetary base, providing liquidity to the real economy, and saw the new monetary aggregate partially replacing the older one.[6] The replacement of cash money by fractional reserve bank money peaked in the late 20th century at 97%. CBDCs are a digital form of money that runs in parallel to cash and the credit money of the commercial banking sector. In future, CBDCs will be 100% backed and run through the traditional commercial banking sector using traditional monetary channels (open-market repos and regular refinancing facilities). However, they will complement rather than replace existing monetary aggregates. CBDCs are public cryptocurrencies underpinned by digital code and blockchains that function like official legal tender, similar to cash and bank money, and can be used without restriction by private and public entities. In addition to these new digital currencies being fully convertible and, like cash, not bearing any interest, central banks will now start to extend their liquidity guarantee to CBDCs while gradually reducing their guarantees for the conventional banking system, including state guarantees as a lender of last resort. Citizens will have access to this new digital monetary aggregate through an e-wallet, currently with a limited volume of 3,000 euros.[7] The anonymity and privacy of CBDCs are similar to bank money, cash or a prepaid card.[8] CBDC users will be able to make payments online or offline by means of near-field communication technology, like with a cashback credit card. A digital smart contract underlying CBDCs makes it possible to configure them to specific targets and projects. Despite the rather technical way in which this new form of money has been introduced, the next step in the evolution of our monetary system will provide some explosive and disruptive potential that will be crucial for the entire Bretton Woods 2.0 agenda. The following aspects are of particular relevance. First, as a new form of liquidity and a new way of channelling money, CBDCs are a perfect candidate to stabilise the monetary system, reducing the risks of bank runs, the pro-cyclical tendency of the traditional commercial banking system and the intrinsic bias towards the FIRE sector that could potentially cause the needs and demands of the real economy to be neglected.[9] This anti-cyclical component to easing and tightening the money supply is of particular interest in times of increasing volatility, contagion effects and cascading domino risks for capital funds, private equity and insurers. This further supports the clear role that central banks play in maintaining price stability. CBDCs also provide an additional public steering and funding tool for common goods and the management of negative externalities and future shocks in cases where private-market activities alone fail to provide adequate resources (Box 5.1).[10]

Box 5.1 The evolution of an additional monetary aggregate

There are two bottom-up developments happening in parallel that support the relevance of an additional monetary aggregate.[11] First, the emergence of cryptocurrencies: there are currently over 2,300 different cryptocurrencies in use, including Bitcoin, Libra, Ethereum and Solana. They all operate in a digital format only, use distributed ledger technology, involve a digital social contract and are issued and created by private 'miners'. Cryptocurrencies are highly capitalised (2.4 trillion USD in 2024)[12] and highly volatile (>5% in 24 hours), yet speculative. The crypto community sees money as a private good with limited liability and favours decentralisation and denationalisation of the monetary sphere.[13] Second, there are over 3,400 complementary non-profit community currency systems operating in 23 countries across six continents. They include Time Dollar systems, local exchange trading systems, local complementary currencies like the Bristol Pound in the UK, the WIR in Switzerland or RegioMoney in Germany and multilateral barter systems. The overall market capitalisation is low and these currencies' macroeconomic impact is next to irrelevant. Yet these thousands of real-time community currencies act like sandbox experiments that prove the relevance of an additional monetary aggregate. They facilitate transactions that might otherwise not have taken place.

I would compare this whole field of evolving parallel currencies today to the moment when the Wright brothers took off in their first plane: a small-scale event whose true significance was to prove that flying was actually possible. If we translate this into the monetary domain, these developments demonstrate the need for an additional monetary aggregate that acts like a counter-cyclical 'rescue boat' and addresses unmet needs. Whether we use a top-down public approach (CBDCs, CBCSs) or a bottom-up one (crypto- or community currencies), we as humans decide how much use we make of each discovery and invention in order to create the society we want to live in.

Over the last three decades, derivatives have been one of the main financial assets used to hedge and manage risks. An only semi-regulated over-the-counter (OTC) market with a nominal value of over 250 trillion USD annually has been offering first, second or even third-tier derivative assets to reduce the risk of failure and pass the hot potato to someone else. Once the risk materialised, there was always someone else who had to pay the bill, which ultimately got passed to the taxpayer. And as long as perceived risks remained local or sectoral, derivatives were a rational choice for hedging microeconomic risks and leveraging diverging expectations. The Anthropocene era, however, has given rise to systemic risks and uncertainties which can no longer be hedged solely using derivatives. Future expectations of the impact of global warming or biodiversity loss are more likely to converge than diverge, leaving the total risk uncovered. This explains the nature of the serial shocks we are all facing. Even if a rational investor thinks they did 'everything right', they will be hit by unexpected consequences of negative feedback loops and fat-tail events with unprecedented cascade effects.[14] In such a situation, instead of reducing risks, we generate further systemic risks and even more costs. The greater that planetary interconnectedness and volatility become, the more rational it will be to abandon derivatives or to regulate them in a better way. For example, if the Vatican decided to switch from brown to green investment, it could clear its balance sheet, but that would not change actual biophysical reality at all. The brown investment would instead be managed by a different institution that the Vatican has no control over and that might be less competent than the old one. The 'hot potato' is still there and the ecological and social impacts remain unchanged. This explains why we need a financial mechanism that overcomes these constraints. Let's look more closely at this complex issue to better understand the rationale behind the argument.

We can apply the same analysis to the polycrisis we are facing. Take the seven trillion USD of global subsidies for the fossil industry. Two trillion of that amount is direct subsidies and five trillion is indirect subsidies, mainly additional healthcare expenditures and degradation of natural resources. The entire fossil industry has an expected EBITA of one trillion USD globally.[15] This further translates into multiple ownerships and contractual obligations to its constituents. At the same time, this seven trillion USD bill represents income, wages and jobs for millions of people. These subsidies are a perfect example of a negative collective externality associated with 'ending fossil fuels'.[16] The question is twofold. First, who is responsible for these externalities? The owner of the fossil site, the producer of fossil derivative products, the investors, the state or the consumer? The answer: we are all responsible. Seen from this angle, it makes next to no sense to reverse-engineer this process and identify single ownerships and responsibilities. The toothpaste is out of the tube and we have to deal with it together. Second, who is going to pay the bill for this global negative collective externality with all its collaterals and spillovers? The same answer: we will all need to, even if we have different levels of responsibility. The Global North, G7 and OECD countries must shoulder more of the burden than the V20 or the Global South. If we all want to phase out from this seven trillion USD bill, we need a monetary mechanism in place that enables us to divide up the collective responsibility, multiple ownerships and obligations. Instead of creating additional hedging instruments, we will need multiple swap agreements.

In the case of the seven trillion USD of fossil subsidies, the oil needs to stay in the ground, but the multiple ownerships, obligations and revenue expectations also need to be respected. We need a mega-scale swap line geared towards keeping fossil fuels in the ground and expediting the reduction of CO_2 emissions to zero. The additional liquidity and compensation required to swap from fossil to green assets would be earmarked so that instead of drilling for oil, a portion of the money would have to be used to build hospitals and nurseries or to plant trees. These swap lines would reflect the obligation to abandon revenue from fossil energy and generate future revenue through green assets alone.[17] Altogether, that would be difficult but doable, given the sophistication of the derivatives market, our first attempt at a mechanism to hedge systemic risks. In order to make this a real deal, we need the regulators to lean in. That is the topic of the next section.

Central Bank Currency Swabs (CBCS) lines are one of the hidden monetary and financial champions that could allow us to meet the funding and hedging needs of our global commons. Technically speaking, a currency swap line is a political agreement between two countries' central banks to exchange their domestic currencies with each other. It represents an inter-regulator exchange between a highly convertible currency (USD, euro) and a weaker one. Most swap lines are capped and bilateral and can help to prevent fire sales and tackle unprecedented shocks. Currency swap lines currently represent up to two trillion USD equivalent that is eligible for settlement between central banks, of which only 300 billion USD equivalent is reserved for developing countries.[18] For example, the Eurozone has established a swap line with the US dollar making it possible to settle the face value of currencies, whereas the Canadian dollar had a capped swap line with Mexico at a value of 240 million CAD and the US had one with Mexico at a value of 15 billion USD in 2023.[19] Theoretically, any country with the sovereignty to print its own money can do so without limits. If a country is indebted in a foreign currency and is facing imported inflation, bilateral or multilateral currency swap lines can be used to tackle this challenge.[20] Take the V20, the most vulnerable countries on this planet and also the ones most affected by climate change. It would be more than rational to increase the swap lines with these countries by a factor of two to three, equivalent to 600 to 900 billion USD. That would be the fastest, least expensive way to provide additional liquidity for specific measures and require the least regulatory effort, as demonstrated by the following case study (Box 5.2).

Box 5.2 Swap lines for the V-20 states facing massive climate change impacts

The V20[21]: the most vulnerable countries are facing disproportionate hazards, with rising floods, wildfires, unreliable rainfall, droughts, water stress and biodiversity loss, food insecurity and health impacts (heat-related deaths, increased dengue and vibrio transmission, malaria outbreaks) combining to drive down GDP per capita, increase lost labour hours, accelerate imported inflation and drive up interest rates and costs of capital for sovereign credit lines. The striking part of this story is that the Global North bears the vast share of responsibility for these challenges and also has all the solutions at hand. CBCS lines would be a fast and precise monetary tool to alleviate the challenges. The final result would be that the balance sheets of central banks in the Global North would increase by the volume of USD equivalent required and the V20 would finally have the drugs, drones and dams that they need and enough money to cover the losses and damage.

As long as central banks and regulators facilitate the fossil-driven economy at a large scale with their current monetary policy, they should extend their mandate to factor in scientific findings on planetary boundaries, resource depletion, biodiversity loss and climate-related issues to stabilise the Consumer Prize Index (CPI) in the future. A green CBDC and its associated swap lines are candidates to serve this function, and would help to level the playing field. Figure 5.3 summarises the entire argument.

We need to transition to a green monetary ecosystem

The findings of the previous sections can be encapsulated in the idea of a monetary ecosystem as part of the Bretton Woods 2.0 agenda. USD supremacy is

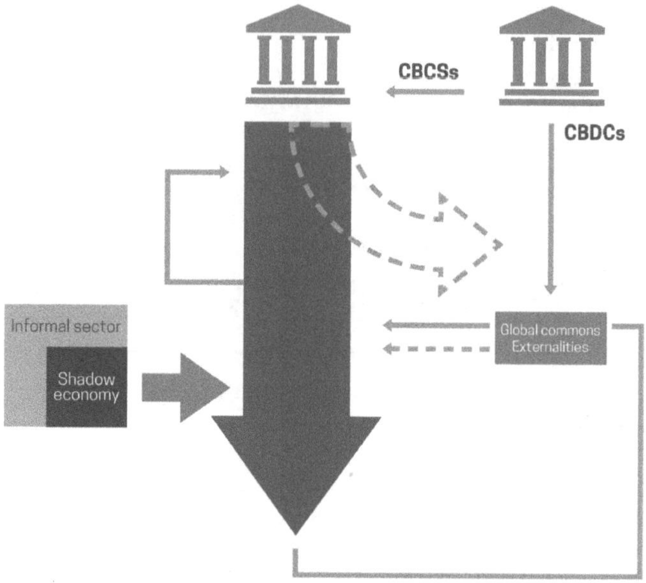

Figure 5.3 Rethinking finance: CBDCs and CBCSs can provide the additional liquidity required to fund, manage and hedge our commons

considered the single most important factor behind global financial instability, but at the same time an anchor for monetary stability. The USD causes debt traps, inflationary pressure and a lack of adequate liquidity on the periphery of the global economy on the one hand while providing a safe haven and a benchmark for investments on the other.[22] There are several caveats to address before we move on. If we take the expected growth rate of BRICS+ countries to be twice that of the G7 and recognise that the Global South requires twice as much investment (4–8% of GDP) as the Global North (2–4% of GDP) and that we need additional, conditioned liquidity to finance our future, the best next step for a greener currency regime will be as follows: within a 'window of opportunity' over the next two decades during which the ecosystem is still fairly intact and nation-states (operating on different, partly conflicting agendas) remain functional, and further assuming that the global market does not become fully fragmented and protectionist and we do not enter a state of global war, regulators and central banks will provide the additional liquidity that is needed by using their sovereign right to create money. This additional monetary supply aggregate would come in a digital format underpinned by blockchain technology and a smart contract that requires that the money only be used for the UN SDGs, thus creating a competitive green marketplace. That would add a green layer denominated in CBDCs or CBCSs, based on the current compositions of major currencies. Globally, this would represent a bill of several trillion USD. The relative future weight and relevance of any currency involved would be determined by the amount of this additional green liquidity.[23] This proposal would further avoid the debate about USD supremacy or any multi-currency basket and make the entire IMS more stable and reliable. And last but not least, it would be relatively easy to implement. We would then end up with a green, long-term, risk-hedged, anti-cyclical, built-in stabiliser that better reflects both the costs and the opportunities we are faced with. And the overall argument still holds that this green monetary ecosystem would transcend the conflicting political agendas of our multipolar world. That might not be obvious at first glance, but it is the definition of madness to repeat business as usual over and over again and expect different results. 'Out of the box' and the 'best next step' seem to be the order of the day. Figure 5.4 summarises these points in terms of the Society for Worldwide Interbank Financial Telecommunication (SWIFT) payment system.[24] The dark grey circles represent the additional liquidity, which is conditioned and can only be used to fund a greener and more inclusive future. This monetary aggregate would provide a steering, funding and stabilising mechanism that is desperately needed.

The circles represent a selection of the most active currencies used for international transactions in 2024 as a proportion of SWIFT payment values. RUB = Russian ruble; CNY = Chinese yuan; GBP = British pound; EUR = euro; USD = US dollar.

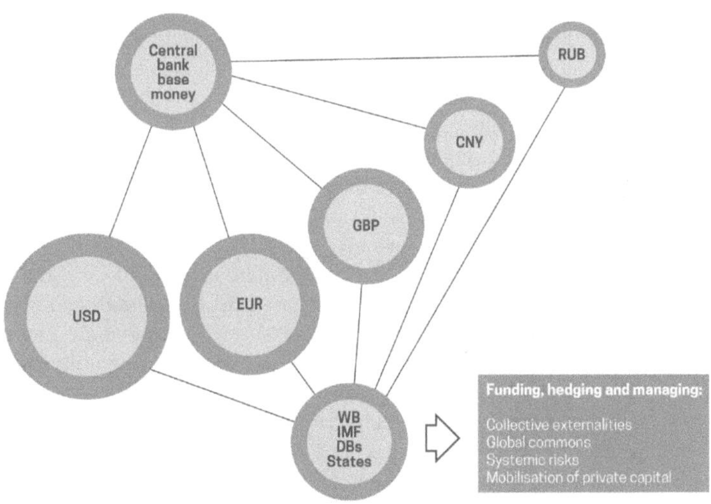

Figure 5.4 Towards a monetary ecosystem: a dual green digital currency system within a multipolar currency world

The dark grey circles represent the required additional, conditioned liquidity provided by central banks through CBDCs or associated swap lines in order to finance and hedge loss and damage funds and global commons so that we can cope with future ecological shocks and provide liquidity for additional financial instruments (hedging, guarantees, etc.) to further mobilise private capital.[25] What impact would this kind of additional, green, conditioned liquidity line have on the conventional economy? It would not be a harmful one; rather, corporate and state planning, production and price levels would become more resilient and reliable with a longer-term vision. Furthermore, the additional liquidity would stabilise the economic cycle of booms and busts in an anti-cyclical manner. Despite arguments to the contrary, we need much more financialisation (finance/GDP). However, that financialisation must be designed in a more democratic and humane manner, so as to protect the planet while increasing wealth for two-thirds of the global population. If there is a single most important variable besides technology, governance, behavioural changes, educational programmes and demographic factors when it comes to changing the world, it is new, digital financial engineering instruments. That would be a real game changer and could be set in motion in less than a year, if the six largest central banks agreed to create an optional, complementary, green currency line. The associated funds would be earmarked and used exclusively to finance SDG-related projects. This electronic liquidity would run through different monetary channels from those of the conventional system. We would then have a supplementary currency operating in parallel to the conventional monetary system, generating the liquidity needed for the next 20 years. For example, this new digital technology could be used to create and channel targeted financial liquidity to millions of people in Africa through their mobile phone network. In India, the existing microcredit banking system could be used to transfer additional liquidity to millions of its citizens or to provide tailored catastrophe bonds (CAT bonds) in case of droughts. Any dollar spent and invested through these green, parallel channels would have the potential to reduce absolute poverty globally. The electronic format would further prevent corruption and fraud, as each transaction would be transparent and public. As the currency could be used to pay taxes, government agencies would have additional liquidity to rebuild public infrastructure, such as nurseries, parks, hospitals and libraries. And the millions of NGOs globally would finally receive the funding they need to do their jobs properly. This targeted additional liquidity would enhance education and provide access to universal healthcare that would otherwise never materialise. It would reduce resource depletion and clean up the air, preventing negative effects on our planet and on public health. Implementing these green CBDCs and CBCSs would help to transform our entire society, whose economy is still 80% fossil-based, into a green marketplace. We would eventually unlock the untapped potential of millions of unemployed people (many of whom are currently active in the informal sector) by creating new jobs, which would in turn unlock the creativity of billions more people. Redesigning the financial system would not solve all our problems, but it would make them easier to address. This, or some similar mechanism, is the missing link to achieving better outcomes in terms of people, prosperity, peace, planet and partnerships. If we want to think outside the box and consider an alternative approach, our financial system will then become pivotal.

If we took up this proposal, we would enter an era where finance no longer drives our common future, but the other way round: an era where our future requirements drive finance. One where nurseries are not run by accountants but by trained educational professionals and hospital chains not by CFOs but by medical directors. Where money is considered not a natural law, but a convention we can change. Where regulators develop the next step in the evolution of money, CBDCs. Where an additional monetary facility provides the funding tools to hedge and manage public goods and public guarantees to mobilise private capital. Where new technologies – AI, big data and distributed ledger technologies – reveal their potential as a force for good and help to adjust our monetary regime with a built-in stabiliser.

We are now in a position to apply all the preliminary findings about a new, upgraded, green Bretton Woods agenda in more detail. That will be the topic of the next chapter.

Notes

1 One of the most striking challenges we are facing here is best described in terms of a 'diffusion of responsibility'. As long as the different levels of regulatory responsibility are not clear, causal attribution will fail. The question of who is in charge will remain unanswered: consumers, investors, states and monetary regulators have different forms of responsibility, which should be aligned.

2 'Effective altruism' is a prominent example (see MacAskill 2017). The argument goes as follows: hedge fund managers could pledge their income to a deworming campaign and do far more good than if they quit their jobs and became organic farmers (cf. Strom 2007). But this approach operates within the existing financial system and assumes that it functions properly when the reality is that it is flawed from the ground up. In short, we need to upgrade the system to meet the requirements of the 21st century, instead of merely working with or around the existing system.

3 Brunnhuber 2021 and 2023; Lietaer, Bernhard (2001).

4 For Nash's original account of the eponymous equilibrium, see Nash 1950 or Brunnhuber 2021.

5 Atlantic Council 2024.

6 See Ferguson 2008.

7 A waterfall effect will automatically convert any additional digital euros into conventional banking money. This design will protect the commercial banking system's fractional use of credit lines and limit high-volume use of any CBDCs. China, the

UK and Sweden have similar technical restrictions built into the design of their first-generation CBDCs. The EU CBDC is due to be launched in 2026/27.

8 Huber 2024; Kumhof and Noone 2021.

9 While conventional monetary easing has been too slow and ineffective in times of crisis, a monetary regime that uses CBDCs makes the ambiguous role of interest adjustment less relevant and provides a more effective approach to public funding, all in line with Article 104 of the Maastricht Treaty (Egmond and Vries 2024).

10 Desan 2022; Jackson and Dyson 2012; Tamez et al. 2024.

11 See also Brunnhuber 2021 and 2023.

12 Statistics.com (2024).

13 These relate to 'decentralised finance' (DeFi), where business models allow transactions without intermediaries such as banks. A token, created for instance by an initial coin offering and linked to a blockchain-based smart contract, provides this additional liquidity needed for the transaction. At present, DeFi business models have a volume of almost 50 billion TVL (total value locked) and remain a niche product. Fully decentralised finance is a myth. Creating and maintaining any DeFi models will always require some sort of hierarchy. All DeFi models to date have failed because they (often surreptitiously) involved some sort of centralised finance (CeFi). The defaults of the crypto stock exchange FTX, the stablecoin TerraUSD and the crypto bank Celsius are recent examples. Meyer et al. 2022; EU Blockchain Observatory and Forum 2024. Instead of further decentralising the financial and monetary system, we should start by upgrading it.

14 Risks then not only multiply but transfer to other less obvious sectors, such as food supply, health/public infrastructure and non-climate drivers. See European Environment Agency 2024.

15 See Bevilacqua et al. 2024.

16 For example, as long as over 50% of the world's population is still dependent on synthetic fertilisers, and hence on fossil energy, to produce their daily food, stopping fossil fuels would push millions of people into famine and poverty with devastating consequences. We clearly need an entirely different perspective on how to phase out fossil fuels.

17 To be more precise: because approximately 78 companies account for 71% of the global carbon footprint, the CEOs of these companies should be given an executive incentive to phase out and shut down as fast as possible and to build up alternative investments for shareholders instead. See Carbon Majors 2024.

18 There are currently no swap lines between the US or EU and African countries, while China is reported to have (mostly undisclosed) swap lines with over 32 countries. See Council on Foreign Relations 2024.

19 The IMF's special drawing rights are a special case. Over 95% of the 982 billion SDRs (as of 2023) are used by OECD countries and MICs. See Setser and Paduano 2022.

20 Access to bilateral swap lines is mainly restricted to OECD countries. 99% of least developed countries (LDCs), 95% of landlocked developing countries (LLDCs) and small island developing states (SIDSs) and 70% of middle-income countries (MICs) have no access to such agreements. See Perks et al. 2021.

21 Established in 2015 during the annual meeting of the World Bank and the IMF, the V20 represents the most vulnerable states facing the impact of climate change. It now has 68 member states and represents a total of 1.7 billion people, a combined GDP of 3.8 trillion USD and 5% of world emissions. See Vulnerable Twenty Group (V 20) 2024.

22 The argument for a currency basket with multiple currencies is a source of instability too, as the volatility of the exchange rate is self-reinforcing and it will take decades before most currencies can be traded without any capital controls. See Gallagher and Kozul-Wright 2022.

23 Technically speaking, this would require a bifurcation of the interest rate (brown versus green). The spread would then reflect the added risk–return premium. Currency carry traders would hedge between these two spreads, carrying the risks during their transactions and could help to dampen the volatility in the currency market.

24 SWIFT has over 11,500 members and a daily trading volume of over 34 trillion USD. See SWIFT 2024.

25 This is partly in line with the proposal of Hiebert and Monnin 2023, who call for a systemic risk buffer (Sy-RB) to cover the potential future costs.

6 Upgrading the system

Towards a green Bretton Woods

To quote Mahatma Gandhi: 'The difference between what we do and what we are capable of doing would suffice to solve most of the world's problems.' And the International Monetary System (IMS) is capable of doing a great deal. In this chapter, I will outline some of the major reforms to the IMS that are needed so that we can operate in a multipolar world with conflicting political agendas, tackle the global ecological crisis and use new, emerging technologies in a way that serves the good of humankind. My main aim is to set out a comprehensive new monetary architecture that allows us, first, to mobilise private capital; second, to fund, hedge and manage our planetary commons; and third, to scale up new technologies. This new architecture would be better able to cope with collective externalities and systemic risks. I will also outline a preliminary financial transition plan and suggest some out-of-the-box financial engineering instruments to better manage the challenges ahead. The big takeaway is that we need far more liquidity in the market. Austerity is over. The overall argument is structured around the new and more prominent role that central banks, regulators and treasuries will play. We need to be guided by a narrative that explains why the overall monetary system should act anti-cyclically and preventively rather than on an ad hoc, ex post basis. We need it because rejecting an updated IMS will be too expensive for all of us. Simply put: transforming the IMS is worth the effort. While all the obvious and traditional measures – in particular green taxonomies, taxation schemes, debt restructuring, green savings accounts, loss and damage funds and philanthropic pledges – do have value in and of themselves and can help to drive specific political actions, investment strategies or consumption patterns, I shall be making the case for new institutional and systemic incentives. In short: polity needs to take precedence over politics. Although the list is incomplete, I would propose at least the following measures:

- Extended role for regulators.
- A public central clearing counter-party (PCCP) for derivatives.
- Foreign Direct Investments (FDIs) and a reformed investment court system (ICS).

DOI: 10.4324/9781003499978-6

- A reformed supply chain act.
- Reforms to rating agencies.
- Reformed voting powers at international monetary institutions.

Extended role for regulators

The core task of any new, upgraded, green Bretton Woods 2.0 agenda would be focused not on regulating the market or intervening in sovereign states' laws and self-determination, but rather on identifying the most suitable regulators for the IMS and reintroducing a regulatory framework for the regulators themselves. The primary goal is not to constrain private initiatives, but rather to correct inefficient, irresponsible and misdirected financial incentives. That requires us, first, to mobilise private capital and domestic savings[1] and move away from a situation where private companies reap insanely high levels of pro-cyclical, short-term windfall profits and leave the public sector to clean up the mess afterwards. Second, it requires us to address and hedge systemic risks and support governments to fund and manage our global planetary commons. Third, the monetary prerequisites must be put in place for funding to scale up all the new technologies we already have at hand. This will help us progress towards a greener and more inclusive future and enable us to cope with all the negative collective externalities, asymmetric shocks, backlashes, tipping points and spillovers. The ultimate result would not be a reduced role for the private sector, but rather more, better and more efficient market solutions, and not a reduced role for the public sector, but rather more preventive and proactive government initiatives. The IMS would then serve as a global public good, providing a comprehensive, collectively shared and approved framework, rather than a casino where outcomes are determined by risky bets and (good or bad) luck. In short: more market and more government, but done differently and leading to an overall reduction in harm.

In the previous chapters, I attempted to apply systems thinking to the IMS, so as to provide us with out-of-the-box solutions. Instead of further fragmenting and decentralising the monetary system and looking at the smallest common denominator, we should upgrade it. One of the core ideas of this book is that we are in need of additional, conditioned liquidity that operates on different monetary channels than those we are used to. Measures such as CBDCs, CBCSs and green QE could serve that purpose. Central banks would have to adapt their internal accounting. Rather than providing loans and credit lines to the public sector, they would hold assets equal to their liabilities and equities. Their balance sheets would then extend accordingly. This would enable us to install a green monetary ecosystem, built upon the existing US Dollar (USD) supremacy but adding additional, conditioned liquidity and incentives to the market. Unlike Bretton Woods 1.0, where capital controls provided some sort of stability, Bretton Woods 2.0 should favour conditioning over controlling. Meaning that footloose capital would remain untouched, but would not benefit from any bailouts in the event of a default. If private capital becomes vested in domestic markets and requires public agencies to hedge associated systemic risks and uncertainties, the liquidity provided by the public sector would come with a condition attached: it can only be invested in certified green assets.[2] I call this monetary facility COLA: *conditioned liquidity assistance*. It would be issued by public regulators and provide additional money in the form of swaps, direct funds, grants, credit lines, equity shares or public guarantees. Its main purpose is to unlock private capital and allow us to manage our commons and hedge systemic risks. For planetary commons, COLA could take the form of 'net-zero-coupon perpetual facilities', where one public body (the regulator) provides liquidity assistance for another (the government or any Intergovernmental Organization (IGO) to manage public goods. These facilities would be wholly digital and utilise distributed ledger technology and, potentially, smart contracts. This would decrease fraud and corruption, increase traceability and help investors meet their targets more reliably. Multilateral Development Banks (MDBs) would become key players, since they have the expertise and knowledge but, at present, often lack adequate funding.[3] COLA would equip them far better to serve their purpose. Besides providing conventional credit lines, which have to be paid back, MDBs would far more easily be able to provide development facilities based on public–private partnerships; they could become official ODA donors, acting as intermediaries and only hedging the systemic risks; they could provide equity shares to companies and offer additional subsidies, transfer payments and grants to support domestic projects; and they could provide far better technical support, build capacity far more effectively, issue green bonds and implement other financial engineering instruments (Box 6.1).

Box 6.1 Open banking for MSMEs to bridge the funding gap

One prominent example is the funding gap of over five trillion USD for the 160 million micro-, small and medium-sized enterprises (MSMEs) worldwide. Three-quarters of MSMEs do not even have access to bank loans. This is a sign of capital market inefficiency. High interest rates, complex administrative procedures and a lack of collateral mean millions of companies cannot access adequate liquidity. The concept of 'open banking', where financial institutions have direct access to the balance sheet (data in motion principle), can reduce costs, increase trust and reliability, generate massive quantities of bottom-up alternative data and allow secondary debt market scaling (mortgage-backed securities).[4]

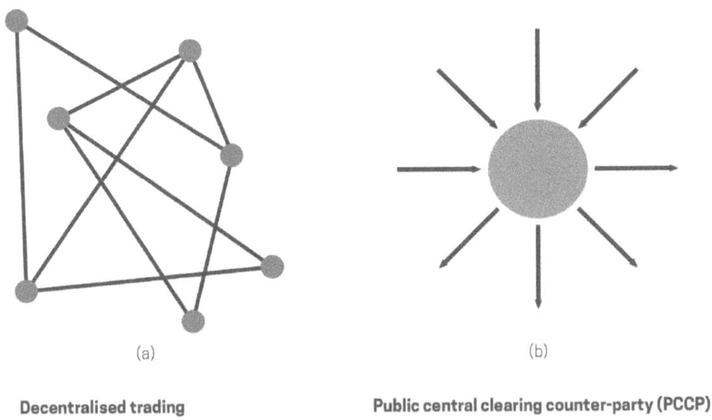

Figure 6.1 Decentralised trading (a) versus a public central clearing counter-party (PCCP). (b) If any agent in (a) comes under stress, the entire network will be affected.

A public central clearing counter-party for derivatives

In a general sense, a clearing house allows buyers and sellers to settle transactions without any direct contracts between them. The clearing house serves as an intermediary between multiple parties, which reduces default risks, enables independent evaluation and monitoring of each party's creditworthiness, reduces the collateral deposits and guarantees funding in the event of a default. If structured as a public central clearing counter-party (PCCP), it would in addition provide an essential mechanism to increase the transparency and stability of the IMS, preventing contagion/domino effects and reducing systemic risk for third parties, especially in the case of CDOs and CDSs. Figure 6.1 illustrates the difference between a decentralised, unregulated, Over the counter (OTC) transaction model and a PCCP.

In a decentralised, non-regulated market (a), participants are exposed to systemic risks above and beyond their project risks, even though they may not have caused those systemic risks themselves. Especially in cases of defaults involving complex financial assets, reverse engineering becomes impossible and multiple uncollateralised systemic risks are created that will ultimately have to be covered by the public sector and the taxpayer. A PCCP (b) can overcome this market flaw by providing the means and liquidity to cover part of the systemic risk, thus allowing market participants to better hedge and assess their own activities. It would not replace hedging instruments like Credit Default Swabs (CDSs), Collateral Debt Obligations (CDOs), swaps or Asset Backed Securities (ABSs), but rather reduce the costs (including those that would ultimately fall on the public purse) in the event of a chain reaction. Designed the right way, a PCCP would create a trade-off between decentralised OTC transactions and transactions that run through the clearing house. These qualified transactions would be safer and less risky, but subject to the condition that they can only be used to fund and invest in green assets. On the other side, OTC products would not be abandoned, but the investor would bear the full responsibility in the event of a default; this would be passed along in the form of higher premiums. Unregulated special investment vehicles, multiple conduits and off-sheet and offshore transactions would then bear the full risk, with no option of a public-sector bailout.[5] This approach would avoid sanctions and additional regulation for OTC products while creating a positive incentive to invest in greener, safer assets, instead of liquidating the hedging market as a whole (Box 6.2).

Box 6.2 The securitisation market 2.0

Let us consider the securitisation market in general and ABSs in particular. ABS products, even though they only represent less than 1% of global investment portfolios, allow us to pass the hot potato to someone else and clear our balance sheet, but they do not address the systemic uncertainties as such. A common global data depository, with shared documentation, templates and standardised products, could indeed help to make the market more efficient, but as we saw in previous chapters not necessarily more resilient. And more transparency can help to further diversify the risk, but not to make the system more stable. As we are facing negative collective systemic externalities and serial asymmetric shocks, it is only with blended finance – where regulators, international financial institutions and MDBs are involved – that the overall systemic risk assessment becomes less uncertain and more reliable. This would further allow an adjusted portfolio that differentiates between vertical (scaling in volume), horizontal (tokenisation) and synthetic (public–private partnerships) ABSs, where first-loss tranches and waterfall effects are clearly defined. These new green ABSs would then run through a PCCP that is preloaded with COLA provided by regulators and treasuries. Only then will the securitisation market be able to fully unlock its market allocation potential and fund, hedge and manage any risks and uncertainties that lie ahead.

The specific example of a PCCP reveals a more general principle about the public sector. If public agents engage in the capital market themselves, this can (as is well known) create crowding-out effects. So increasing public demand for loanable funds drives up the interest rate, which in turn increases opportunity costs for the private sector to make additional investments and thus reduces private-sector involvement. The currency involved appreciates, which attracts foreign capital nominated in that currency and crowds out exports in that currency.[6] However, if the public agent reduces systemic risks using an additional monetary aggregate (e.g., green QE, CBDCs or CBCSs, as explained above) that operates in parallel to the credit market, and this additional liquidity is conditioned to hedge systemic risks, the opposite will occur: private capital formation will 'crowd in'[7]: that is to say, this mechanism would unlock the private capital that is so desperately needed. PCCPs could also use fintech (in particular AI, big data and blockchains) to make more accurate predictions of risks and uncertainties, detect fraud, analyse markets and automate compliance processes, which would further reduce the overall costs involved.

Foreign Direct Investments (FDIs) and a reformed investment court system

FDIs have an important role to play in the green transition but are beset by thorny problems. Globally, they have a total value of about 1.3 trillion USD annually. Over two-thirds of that total remains within rich developed countries. And again, the devil is in the detail. The paradox is that, on the one hand, FDIs do not necessarily trigger domestic growth, but rather tend to crowd out local players. They compete with domestic investments and local banks when it comes to funding local projects. Accordingly, policymakers would be better advised to invest in education and domestic SMEs and banks, rather than providing special conditions for international investors. Especially for emerging markets, there is a clear link between domestic inequality and the level of FDI in the country. On the other hand, the international data on FDIs is to some extent a misleading statistical artefact. Large companies often reroute their money through offshore locations. 30–50% of US and UK investors and up to 80% of Russian ones use this investment loop. According to International Monetary Fund (IMF) data, up to 40% of global FDIs are simply private capital, with special-purpose vehicles running through offshore sites without any real, relevant economic impact. Another way to make this point is by asking: who are the UK's, the USA's and Russia's biggest foreign investors? The answer, respectively, is the UK, the USA and Russia themselves.[8] These black loops do not create any additional common value but rather serve as tax avoidance strategies.[9]

Under the current set of rules, countries can be sued by private investors if state actions negatively affect private investments. International arbitral tribunals protect FDIs through almost 3,000 bilateral investment treaties, assorted multilateral agreements and the Transatlantic Trade and Investment Partnership. They provide security, 'free transfer of means' and legal protection for foreign investors against expropriation. For example, domestic laws designed to protect the environment introduce a minimum wage or address public health issues could be subject to ICS proceedings if investors feel they have been negatively affected and seek compensation. The current legal framework of the ICS comprises treaties between countries that protect investors located in those countries. The ICS only allows private investors to sue states, not the other way round, which puts the public sector in a defensive role. Introducing and holding on to this two-tier legal system, where domestic regulations and international investment rules are decoupled, poses a challenge for democracies.[10] There is increasing evidence that the ICS needs to be reformed. It is inconsistent, unfair and lacks transparency and integrity.[11] Private investors should not only be protected against expropriation but also respect democratic decisions. At its core, the existing regulatory framework prevents both states and investors from achieving a sustainable future. This creates endless dilemmas and means that policies like smoking bans, minimum wages and ESG standards are not implemented, despite the obvious need for them and approval from all sides. Nation states are caught in a state of 'regulatory chill' or 'wait and see'[12] – anticipating potential private claims for damages and unable to make progress. At some point, the entire process becomes problematically circular: a state anticipates being successfully sued by an international investor over a new policy and, factoring in this opportunity cost, refrains from implementing it. It's like a game of Mikado: the person who moves first loses.

There are three options: business as usual, exiting the ICS or making some sensible reforms. I favour the last option. Wherever the public interest is at stake, we need an adjusted regulatory framework that on the one hand guarantees and protects investors' (property) rights, but on the other has the flexibility to ensure the state's 'right to regulate' in accordance with approved ESG standards. To break this 'Mikado' deadlock where the first person to move would lose the game, public agents should be provided with upfront, conditioned liquidity to hedge systemic risks associated with the investment. At the same time, the international investor should be acquainted with approved ESG standards that could be adopted over time and do not entitle them to claim damages.[13] Monitoring this process is relatively straightforward because the currency operates solely on digital channels. International investors and companies can prove their sincere interest in the region in question by paying their wages in this parallel green currency and phantom foreign investments will be eliminated little by little.

A reformed supply chain act

International competitive markets are based on a discovery process, where agents voluntarily cooperate to the benefit of both sides. The price signal represents the value of a good or service and ownership rights are resettled. Operating in an unknown territory requires a lot of skill, experience, determination and expertise in such settlements. Local cultural customs, geographic particularities and domestic regulatory frameworks determine whether these efforts succeed or fail. A settled agreement is the result of a complex process that reflects an enormous amount of information and trust, built up over time and distance. Trillions of international transactions occur every day across the globe. Efforts are underway to implement environmental and human rights standards along these global supply chains.[14] We are currently trying to solve these challenges by increasing documentation, regulation and sanctions, which will make the entire supply chain ineffective, inefficient and expensive and result in a legal framework that is anything but fit for purpose. The regulatory efforts do not deliver the expected benefits.[15] Seen from a different, more systemic angle, the collective externalities we are facing along multiple supply chains globally do not necessarily reflect a genuine market failure, but rather a lack of a proper, functioning market, where liabilities, ownership rights, corporate laws and symmetric information would provide a more adequate price signal. In most cases, the company is not the cause of the externality but rather indirectly takes advantage of the wage arbitrage it provides. We should aim for an adjusted supply chain that respects private investments, harnesses the benefits of international labour specialisation, prevents misuse and makes it possible to better hedge and manage the associated collective externalities. For example, suppose a mid-sized European company has built up a supply chain over the last few years so that it can assemble an engine in Europe and operates a manufacturing site in a sub-Saharan country. At this site, a 16-year-old female worker is contracted in a logistics division, earning an hourly income of 1.50 euros below the minimum wage approved between the two countries. Under the current set of rules, the company would consider abandoning its commitment to this logistics unit, because of the higher regulatory and documentation burden, potential claims for damages and additional labour costs that are collectively supposed to cover this negative social externality. The 16-year-old would then eventually lose her job, potentially end up doing sex work and not be able to go to college. At best, the European company would be replaced by a Russian or Chinese one that offers her an alternative job. This 'reshoring' process means that the European company withdraws its investment and suffers harm to its business, while human rights abuses simply continue out of sight. An adjusted supply chain act could do more good and avoid further harm. In that case, the initial supply chain would remain in place, guaranteeing human rights standards, but the associated negative social externality would be covered in part by a green monetary facility provided by the European Investment Bank (EIB), with the domestic MDB operating as an intermediary to transfer the money. That would completely change the playing field. The company would request (part of) the 1.50 euros per hour needed to cover the wage shortfall for the 16-year-old worker from the EIB, the worker herself would provide proof of enrolment at her local college and the additional liquidity would boost the local economy, creating additional purchasing power that is desperately needed.

A final point: the money for this monetary facility would not come from a fiscal squeeze, nor from a public credit line provided to the international capital market, but rather from the monetary creation process that any public central bank is entitled to carry out or from COLA, as explained in the previous chapter. I am aware that the argument may seem redundant in many ways. But we need to generate additional, conditioned liquidity and fund solutions to our global challenges. If regulators or central banks were to provide that liquidity, they would enlarge their balance sheet with a 'zero-coupon perpetual facility' or similar monetary entity, whereby money is earmarked to manage future costs that we have already incurred. If we do this the right way, it will ultimately turn a global supply chain into a true global value chain that serves the common good.

Reforms to rating agencies

One of the major systemic flaws inherent to the IMS concerns rating agencies. Rating agencies have a regulatory function, as they evaluate and predict companies and countries' relative credit risks, potential defaults and the creditworthiness of structured finance (ABSs, CDOs). The agencies are meant to reduce the information asymmetry and provide reliable, objective and independent data so that borrowers can take a preventive, anti-cyclical, foresighted approach. However, their inherently flawed design constantly creates the wrong incentives. Some of these inherent flaws are of particular relevance to the IMS. *Oligopolies:* There are three companies that between them control over 95% of the market.[16] Oligopolies of this kind become market makers with no real competition. *Conflicts of interest:* Rating agencies are profit-seeking private companies. They are paid by the customers they evaluate, which makes the rating process ineffective, inaccurate and expensive for the entire IMS. Instead of preventing debt crises, they potentially accelerate them.[17] As long as the issuer of bonds pays the rating agency, it will benefit from a higher rating, which defeats the purpose. This problem comes particularly to the fore in the design of structured financial assets. Private rating agencies are themselves engaged in the design of collateral debt obligations and complex ABSs, which they then subsequently rate to generate additional revenue.[18] *Acting pro-cyclically:* Instead of counterbalancing the business cycle, the agencies tend to reinforce it in both directions and further exacerbate financial volatility so that a self-fulfilling prophecy negates governments' efforts to address systemic crises. *Lack of accountability:* In the event of a default, credit rating agencies do not provide expert liability and the purpose of the entire rating process is defeated, making it esoteric and expensive overall.[19]

In other words: credit rating agencies are systemically important,[20] but under- or misregulated. They influence investors' portfolio management, interest rates for debt repayments and the flow of international capital. In the face of this toxic mixture of minimal accountability, private profit-seeking, obvious conflicts of interest, pro-cyclical tendencies and the fact that the international credit rating market is basically an oligopoly with next to no competition, there are essentially two ways to reform these activities[21]: we could either re-regulate each of the adverse components of the rating process or create a public entity that is able to manage the task. An intermediary step would be a public–private partnership, where the expertise of both sides is pooled to counteract the flawed design. Applying this argument to a Bretton Woods 2.0 agenda, there are three options we could consider. First, reverse the billing. When it comes to evaluating debtors' ability to meet their debt obligations, instead of having the borrower pay the bill for the rating it should be the lender that pays to get valid information about where they are putting their money. Another fast and cheap intermediary step would be to establish a market solution. A future credit rate swap market could provide immediate, albeit relatively volatile information. A longer-term option would be to introduce an additional public agency that provides credit rating data to companies and countries and competes with the private sector to deliver the best service. Especially when it comes to evaluating systemic risks associated with climate change, negative collective externalities and the role of our planetary commons, the results are more than uninspiring. I believe generative AI and big data analysis can provide the tools to improve both competitiveness and the quality of data. Figure 6.2 illustrates this point.

Reforming voting powers at international monetary institutions

Instead of pursuing a more comprehensive, globally approved consensus on how to address increasing instability and volatility in the IMS, which in turn translates into real physical and economic hazards, there is growing fragmentation of the global mechanisms designed to ensure financial security. This is the result of declining mutual trust and conflicting political agendas in a multipolar world. Four main trends can be observed. First, a rise in regional financial security measures, such as the European Stability Mechanism

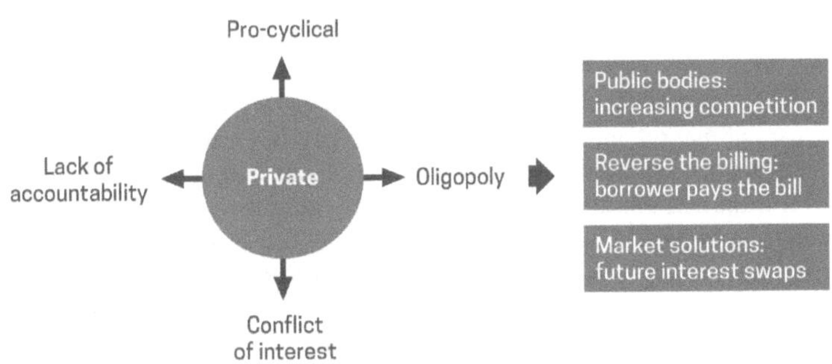

Figure 6.2 Overcoming rating agencies' flawed design

(over 550 billion USD), the Chiang Mai Initiative (250 billion USD) and the BRICS Group (starting with 100 billion USD, which will be expanded in the medium term to include the UAE and Saudi Arabia). Second, an increase in central bank swap lines and repurchase agreements (repos). China alone has settled over 550 billion USD over the last few years using currency swap lines with over 40 countries. Third, the accumulation of foreign currency reserves, worth over 12 trillion USD (2024), of which over 60% (7.5 trillion USD) are held by emerging and developing countries. Fourth, a fragmentation in international banking transactions. China has introduced CIPS (Cross-Border Interbank Payment System), Russia SPFS (Financial Messaging System) and India UPI (Unified Payments Interface), all of which are designed as alternatives to the traditional SWIFT system in order to break with USD supremacy. These trends reflect a general recognition and awareness of future shocks, hazards and instabilities, and underscore the need to provide additional liquidity to address all these challenges. So the question is still unanswered: are these fragmented approaches an adequate response to ever-increasing uncertainties and risks? The current fragmentation of safety-net arrangements could turn out to be, at least in part, a feasible and comprehensive decoupling strategy in order to cope with serial risk cascades, domino effects and systemic ecological shocks – but only if these reform agendas incorporate the new role for regulators that I argue for in this book. Finding the right balance between economic power, shared but different responsibilities and greater efficiency, coordination and political representation is at the heart of the current debate on reforming international financial institutions. In short, a fractured real economy associated with a fragmented IMS will add additional costs to the system and could reduce potential future costs in the event of hazards materialising. Below, I will look at proposed reforms to the three traditional Bretton Woods institutions: the World Bank, the IMF and the World Trade Organization (WTO).

The *World Bank Group*, established in 1944, is an international public bank that is run like a cooperative with 189 stakeholders/members. It was set up with a dual mission: to eliminate poverty globally and to promote sustainable development. It is composed of five institutions, including a large research unit.[22] Voting powers are based on the shares each country holds in the bank.[23] The bank primarily raises the money it lends from the capital market and through fees, shares and interest payments. Its total commitments, including public guarantees, loans and grants, amounted to 145 billion USD in 2023, and it is currently aiming to stretch the balance sheet by another 125 billion USD. That still only represents a fraction of the amount needed to tackle poverty and climate issues annually.[24] The Private Sector Investment Lab[25] is intended to streamline the lending process and make it more transparent. Its goals are to triple the annual guarantee issuance from 6.8 billion USD to 20 billion USD by 2030 and to consolidate the 20 different forms of public guarantees into a single 'menu' (at present, these guarantees represent not even 5% of exposed lending[26]). Another proposed measure is to mobilise private investments and domestic savings and frontload MDBs to secure systemic risk through multiple hedging or equity instruments. For every dollar spent by MDBs, only 0.6–0.7% of that amount in private capital is mobilised (2023). The target should be about eight to ten times higher. Finally, the bank wants to maintain its AAA rating while at the same time factoring in climate risks and promoting poverty reduction goals.[27]

The IMF was founded in 1944 to increase international monetary cooperation and financial stability and to encourage global trade, economic growth, employment and productivity through monitoring, recommendations and adjustment programmes for its 190 members. Its current resources amount to about 982 billion special drawing rights (SDRs), equivalent to about the same number in USD, and come from member quotas and multi- or bilateral borrowing agreements. Each member's quota determines their voting power at the IMF. In its current version (the entire process is currently under negotiation), the quota considers a country's GDP, its openness to trade and the foreign currency reserves held by its central bank. It allows member states to borrow up to 200% annually and up to 600% in total.[28] Each member has 250 basic votes plus SDRs, with one vote equalling 100,000 SDRs. The US ranks relatively low on this variable, which does not reflect USD supremacy given that the Fed acts as a lender of last resort. The criterion of an economy's openness reflects the situation under the initial Bretton Woods regime when trade of goods and services predominated. Since 1980, the financial sector has become a far more dominant factor in the stability of the IMS. If GDP were measured in terms of purchasing power parity (PPP), it would upgrade the Global South to almost 60% of quota power. However, it would not take into account the relative weight of these countries in real international economic transactions.[29] This point underscores the capacity of the Global South to contribute to the stability of the financial system. If we start considering climate change, the picture becomes even more complicated. Given that the largest global cumulative emitters of CO_2 are at the same time the most powerful member states of the IMF,[30] it seems obvious that environmental impact needs to be factored in. In particular, more voting powers should be given to countries that are the most heavily impacted by the crisis yet the least responsible for causing it. The whole process should be reevaluated, based on cumulative carbon emissions[31] weighted by population as a fair measure. Given the global financial gap of several trillion USD annually, with adaptation costs equal to at least 10% of that amount needed by 2023,[32] the IMF's SDRs have a key role to play as a monetary facility. One proposal is to increase the voting share of the Global South to over 50% and that of the V20 (most vulnerable countries, primarily small island developing states (SIDSs)) from 2.5% to 21% while reducing the US's voting share from over 16% to 5.65%.[33]

The WTO was the third organisation to emerge out of the initial Bretton Woods meeting. It was founded in 1995 as a successor to the General Agreement on Tariffs and Trade (GATT) and has not been updated since. The Trade Policy Review Mechanism (TPRM) is supposed to adapt national trade policy to international requirements. The increase of bilateral agreements has made global trade more opaque and complicated. Driven by the overarching idea that free-trade flows stimulate domestic growth and prosperity for all, the WTO has 166 members representing 98% of all global trade activities. The WTO acts as a legally binding mediator to deal with unfair subsidies, trade barriers, intellectual property violations and disputes among trading partners. So far, over 60 binding and enforceable trade agreements have increased transparency, predictability and stability for all parties.[34] The WTO has a budget of 200 million USD, with the USA (11.6%), China (10.8%) and Germany (7.2%) as the three largest donors.[35] The main criticism of the WTO is that it takes trade liberalisation as a general rule, but developing markets need to be able to protect their domestic economies to avoid being unfairly disadvantaged in the face of global competition. The trading environment has changed fundamentally since the WTO was founded. The rise of e-commerce and cybercrime, the digital divide, serial ecological shocks that threaten the global value chain, the disconnect between the financial system and real trading activities and the need to fairly integrate emerging and developing markets into the global trading system are all challenging the free-trade principle.[36]

The current set of rules for international financial institutions faces two additional challenges. First, there is a substantial overlap between the three institutions' agendas, particularly with regard to climate change and the instability of the system. Second, the current mandate can be easily overstretched and locked into a siloed system dilemma: *we know that everything is connected to everything else and that any silo approach could negatively affect the entire system, but we do not have the mandate to change the system to overcome that dilemma*. The Bretton Woods systems are simply not holistic enough to tackle the challenges of the 21st century. Whether voting powers are grouped around population or nation-based measures, cumulative or current CO_2 emissions or favour purchasing power parities or an international USD, each proposal will leave us with two foundational challenges: how to mobilise and hedge private capital, and how to finance and manage our global commons. Honouring what we have already achieved, acknowledging both our institutional limits and our planetary boundaries, criticising oversights or deficiencies in the current system and then moving beyond the status quo towards a better common future seems to be a reasonable common narrative. We need an approach where institutions become more holistic and less hermetic, more systemic and less siloed. If we consider the current process of reforming the Bretton Woods institutions in the face of new realities, the best next step could be grouped around five principles, which are summarised in Table 6.1.

Table 6.1 The five Fs for a Bretton Woods 2.0

	WB	*IMF*	*WTO*
A	Frontloading of additional funds	Reform of special drawing rights (SDRs), adding new financial engineering instruments	Revising the current budget and donor contributions
B	Eradicating poverty	Facing increasing financial instability	E-commerce, global value chains, ecological crisis
C	Adjusted voting quotas that reflect the power game of a multipolar world	Adjusted quotas that reflect the role of LDCs and sustainability issues	New general trade agreements that incorporate the Global South
D	Inclusive development and regional/cultural particularities	Financial stability and providing additional liquidity	Global trade and domestic growth
E	Ecological shocks and poverty	Ecological shocks and stability	Ecological shocks and trade

A: funding; B: fitness for purpose; C: framing; D: facilitating; E: focusing on a common agenda.

Notes

1 There are several options to mobilise private domestic savings. The French government introduced a green 'livret d'épargne populaire' (LEP). People up to the age of 21 can pay up to 30,000 euros into this account tax-free and benefit from a higher interest rate and state guarantee. They can only cash in the money when they turn 21. In an extended version, all citizens are allowed to participate. Insurers and banks collect the money and select the green assets. The ceiling means that large parts of the population can benefit. For example, Germany has eight billion euros in gross savings, with over 40% in cash deposits.

2 If we took this argument one step further, we would end up with a dual currency system, where a green euro, dollar or pound complements the conventional currency and pulls our society towards a greener, more inclusive future. See Brunnhuber 2021 and 2023.

3 See Marois et al. 2024.

4 See People-Centered Internet 2023.

5 See Soros 2009. Note also Warren Buffett's description of derivatives in 2003 as 'financial weapons of mass destruction', which captures the toxic and explosive nature of these assets (BBC News 2003).

6 Traditionally, the World Bank, the IMF and regional development banks have advised countries to borrow money from abroad, via FDIs, loans or portfolio investments, in order to achieve a higher domestic growth rate. Most literature, however, has chronically ignored the role of the domestic banking sector. The domestic banking sector can generate domestic loans via fractional reserves without relying on foreign denominations. See Werner 2014.

7 Damrich et al. 2022.

8 See also Bermejo Carbonell and Werner 2018.

9 This amounts to 15 trillion USD in corporate money. Luxembourg and the Netherlands hold 50% of that capital. In total, 85% of the entire sum globally is located in just ten countries (see Damgaard et al. 2019).
10 UNCTAD 2015.
11 Anderson and Beaumont 2020.
12 Historically, the first investor protection act dates back to the 1959 agreement between Germany and Pakistan. The rationale was to increase FDI in regions where there was a lack of private investment. Sixty-five years later, the empirical evidence is inconclusive about its economic impact. About one-third of related lawsuits are settled, one-third are won by the private sector and one-third by the public sector. See also Dotzauer 2023.
13 Johnson et al. 2019; Kyla et al. 2022.
14 See the EU regulation on supply chain due diligence: European Commission 2024.
15 As well as additional documentation, we can expect at least two further consequences. First, a regulation-induced market concentration that favours large companies and oligopolies, since smaller companies will not be able to keep up with the additional administrative burden. Second, a sales-related fine assessment where companies will have to cover liabilities and reparation costs downstream along the supply chain. Civil law codes will impose sanctions and penalties on companies that fail compliance management assessments. There is a vast body of literature from clinical and social psychology demonstrating that 'positive reinforcement', rather than punishing and sanctioning, will create an incentive that proactively encourages people and companies to do good. The monetary mechanism described in this book (COLA) aims for intermittent positive reinforcement. For an overview, see Brunnhuber 2021.
16 Fitch Ratings, S&P and Moody's. See Hung et al. 2022.
17 Ferri and Liu 2003; Hau et al. 2013.
18 United Nations 2009.
19 Cf. White 2019 and Malewska 2021.
20 Empirically, the basis point spread of an AAA-ranked asset, compared with a risk-free governmental bond, is about 0.43; for a CCC asset, it is over 700 basis points. See He et al. 2000; Bongaerts et al. 2009.
21 Li 2021.
22 ICSID settles investment disputes; MIGA provides political risk insurance; the IFC mobilises private-sector investment and provides consulting services; the IDA offers zero or low-interest loans and grants; the IBRD provides financial resources for development and policy financing. The latter two organisations have a lending volume of 7.5 billion USD (2023). To date, the World Bank Group has funded over 12,000 development projects.
23 At present, the largest shareholders are the USA (16%), Japan (6.5%), China (4.5%), Germany (4%), France (3.9%), the UK (3.9%), India (3%), Russia (2.8%), Brazil (2.2%) and South Africa (0.9%).
24 See Center for Global Development 2023.
25 See World Bank 2024a.
26 IMF 2023; World Bank 2024b.
27 Another prominent proposal is to create a sixth World Bank Group organisation that facilitates global public goods. See Khanna and Healy 2023.
28 To be more precise, there is a difference between calculated quota shares (CQSs) and actual quota shares (AQSs), which are determined by an internal negotiation process whereby the basic votes are added equally to each country. This then leads to the binding quota shares (BQSs). Any changes to quotas require an 85% majority vote from all members. The Global North, representing 49 countries, has 63% of voting power, while the Global South, representing 141 countries, has a total of 37%.

29 This is because PPP reflects the prices of domestic non-tradable goods and services. See Callen 2024.
30 To be more precise: the top 20 emitters have a 64% vote share. See Gütschow et al. 2021.
31 Hickel 2020.
32 Climate Analytics 2023; UN Environment Programme 2023.
33 On this proposal, advanced economies would transfer 12% of their voting power share to developing economies, while developing countries would increase their share from 5.2% to 18%. In sum, the Global South would increase its cumulative share from 37% to 56%. However, this calculation has its own limits. First, countries like Switzerland and Singapore would come out with a higher share, since financial assets play a more relevant role than real trading activities. Second, the weighting of the calculation by population is questionable. Third, how the Global South can be given additional voting power, given that the money is still denominated in USD, remains an unresolved puzzle, See Beyond Bretton Woods (2024):
34 Empirically, international trade without WTO standards would leave states with 32% higher tariffs for exports. Nicita et al. 2018.
35 World Trade Organization 2023.
36 A second-best step would be an *open plurilateralism*, which would allow binding agreements for subgroups with potential benefits for non-signatories. The GATT was designed with a plurilateral structure of this kind. See Schmucker and Mildner 2023.

7 Conclusion

The full picture

None of the challenges that lie ahead can be solved by our existing institutions and political agendas, nor by single nations and isolated actions alone. We need an 'out-of-the-box' approach that has the necessary speed, scale and mindset, and is capable of replacing ad hoc arrangements with long-lasting alliances.[1] In this book, I have attempted to show how the International Monetary System (IMS) can act as a great leverager and integrator along this journey. Despite the rather technical ways in which new forms of money and new monetary channels have been introduced, the next step in the evolution of our monetary system will provide some explosive and disruptive potential that is crucial for the entire Bretton Woods 2.0 agenda. The IMS is a facilitator that can transcend different political agendas and reconcile opposites, ambiguous empirical findings and conflicting interests into a greater whole where we have common but distinct responsibilities and can overcome institutional impediments. This will enable us to think outside the box so that we can enhance the allocative power of a competitive market system by integrating new and different forms of state intervention; to reconcile and transcend different political agendas, so that we can unlock and de-risk the trillions of dollars in domestic savings accounts and the capital market; and to fund and manage our common public goods.[2] My argument has focused on the prominent role of monetary regulators, addressing the intrinsic structure of the monetary system and its main institutions. The notion of central bank neutrality is a fallacy, as each bond purchasing programme is currently still biased towards brown assets and each intervention on the market has an implicit or explicit distributional impact. I am calling for a paradigm shift that addresses the concrete practices, guiding principles and underlying purpose of the IMS. Bretton Woods 1.0 was not designed to transform our society but rather to provide stability through capital controls and pegged currency regimes. A Bretton Woods 2.0 should pursue a narrative that is sufficiently inclusive ('Nothing about us without us') and holistic ('There is no planet B') to accommodate multipolarity and cultural differences.[3] And it should be an agenda that incorporates the transition itself. Instead of providing capital controls and pegged currency regimes, a Bretton Woods 2.0 should favour a shift from controlling to conditioning

DOI: 10.4324/9781003499978-7

Table 7.1 A preliminary checklist for a Bretton Woods 2.0 moment

The right narrative	East–West, North–South, multidisciplinary, transcultural Reconciling national interests and international resources Sustainability agenda and new systems clash Reconstruction and development Restructuring and external shocks Multilateralism and multipolarity
Hedging systemic uncertainties	Anti-cyclical Managing footloose capital Secondary prevention approach Risks and uncertainties Long-termist and reliable Managing negative collective externalities Public clearing house for derivatives
Resetting the institutional framework	Beyond ad hoc cooperation Sovereignty, leadership and distribution New voting powers for WTO, IMF and WB New liabilities and responsibilities Reforming investor–state dispute settlement (ISDS) Dollar supremacy and currency diversification New mandate for regulators (green CBDCs and CBCSs) Reforms to rating agencies The role of multilateral development banks (MDBs)
Creating purchasing power	Austerity is over Additional, conditioned liquidity assistance (COLA) Financing planetary commons and de-risking private capital Green QE A new supply chain act The role of SDRs and currency swap agreements Debt restructuring and reformed taxation schemes
Four Ts: Technology Taxonomy Transparency Transition plans	Predictive coding and now-casting Big data correlations to tackle complexity ESG standards Tackling illicit transactions, fraud and corruption Shadow banking and shadow economy New financial engineering instruments Open banking

capital, from self-defeating austerity to additional liquidity, from analogue to digital, from repairing the system to preventing damage. Regulators need to integrate biophysical parameters into their equations. That requires additional, conditioned liquidity for their core tasks: deleveraging private capital, funding and managing planetary commons and enabling funding to scale up cross-cutting technologies to support the transition. Table 7.1 summarises the ingredients for an updated, green Bretton Woods and provides a preliminary checklist.

If we take all the arguments presented above together, we have three main options: an *ad hoc scenario*, where we continue muddling through, apply incremental silo solutions but leave the fundamental flaws untouched; a *big leap scenario*, where we wholly reject the Bretton Woods institutions and build a new institution or institutions instead; and a *best next step scenario*, where we leave the current institutions in place, acknowledge the challenges, appreciate what we have achieved, criticise missteps and omissions, correct the perverse incentives and integrate them into a greater whole. But any approach will be a matter of trial and error. The first two scenarios, while appealing, would be too slow, too small in scope and too expensive. It is easy to get bogged down in detailed incremental regulations. And it is somewhat dangerous to advocate a big-picture solution without taking responsibility for its implementation and costs and the potential harm of defaults. Both scenarios would involve additional political and economic opportunity costs that we have to factor in. The *purpose* of a new Bretton Woods agenda is to provide more funding and stability for our common future, the *principles* are based around the new role of regulators and the *practices* are outlined in this book. We could conclude: the long shadow of the past has prevented us from looking to the future. But we humans are not only the most adaptive species on this planet, we are also capable of seeing that we are operating and living within a web without a weaver – and that is forcing us to start thinking outside the box.

Notes

1 World Academy of Art and Science 2024; Human Security for All 2024.
2 Theoretically and empirically, it remains an open question whether economic growth causes savings or savings cause economic growth. This should remind us that complex systems do not follow a linear causal trajectory, but rather proceed along multicausal feedback loops. See Modigliani 1986. Distinguishing between domestic savings and foreign savings could help us resolve the puzzle; see Volz et al. 2024.
3 Bristow et al. 2024.

References

Adger, W. Neil et al. (2022): “Climate Change Affects Multiple Dimensions of Well-Being through Impacts, Information and Policy Responses”, in: *Nature Human Behaviour*, 6, 1465–1473, https://doi.org/10.1038/s41562-022-01467-8.

Adrian, Tobias; Ashcraft, Adrian (2016): “Shadow Banking: A Review of the Literature”, in: *Banking Crises: Perspectives from The New Palgrave Dictionary*, London: Palgrave, 282–315, https://doi.org/10.1057/9781137553799_29.

Adrian, Tobias; Jones, Bradley (2018): “Shadow Banking and Market-Based Finance”, IMF Monetary and Capital Markets Department No. 18/14, https://doi.org/10.5089/9781484343883.087.

Aigner, J. (2019): “The Unstoppable Surge in Negative Yields Reaches $17 Trillion”, *Broadcast by Bloomberg*, 23 December 2019, https://www.bloomberg.com/graphics/negative-yield-bonds/.

Alberti, Caroline (2024): “The Cost of Inaction, Climate Policy Initiative”, https://www.climatepolicyinitiative.org/the-cost-of-inaction/.

Alfonso, António; Tovar Jalles, João; Venâncio, Ana (2023): “Government Spending and Tax Revenue Decentralization and Public Sector Efficiency: Do Natural Disasters Matter?”, cesifo Working Papers 10424, https://ec.europa.eu/economy_finance/arc2023/documents/papers/Afonso%20A.%20-%20Government%20Spending%20and%20Tax%20Revenue%20Decentralization%20and%20Public%20Sector%20Efficiency.pdf.

Anderson, Alan M.; Beaumont, Ben (Eds.) (2020): *The Investor State Dispute Settlement System*, Alphen aan den Rijn: Kluwer Law International.

Atlantic Council (2024): “Central Bank Digital Currency Tracker”, https://www.atlanticcouncil.org/cbdctracker/.

Attridge, Samantha; Engen, Lars (2019), *Blended Finance in the Poorest Countries. The Need for a Better Approach*, London: ODI.

Ayers, Robert (2016): *Energy, Complexity and Wealth Maximization, The Frontiers Collection*, Switzerland: Springer.

Ayres, Robert U. (2016): “Gaps in Mainstream Economics: Energy, Growth, and Sustainability”, in: Shmelev, Stanislav (Ed.): *Green Economy Reader: Lectures in Ecological Economics and Sustainability*, Basel: Springer.

Bainbridge, David A. (2023): *Accountability: Why We Need to Count Social and Environmental Cost for A Livable Future*, New York: Rio Redondo Press.

Bank for International Settlements (2022): “Triennial Central Bank Survey: OTC foreign exchange turnover in April 2022”, Bank for International Settlements 2022, https://www.bis.org/statistics/rpfx22_fx.pdf.

Barman, Emily. (2018), "Doing Well by Doing Good: A Comparative Analysis of ESG Standards for Responsible Investment", in: *Sustainability, Stakeholder Governance, and Corporate Social Responsibility (Advances in Strategic Management, Vol. 38*, Leeds: Emerald Publishing Limited, pp. 289–311. https://doi.org/10.1108/S0742-332220180000038016.

Bazerman, Max H.; Moore, Don A. (2012): *Judgement in Managerial Decision Making*, New York: John Wiley & Sons.

BBC News (2003): "Buffett Warns on Investment 'Time Bomb'". *BBC News*, Tuesday, March 4th 2003, https://news.bbc.co.uk/2/hi/2817995.stm.

Berg, Florian; Kölbel, Julian F., Rigobon, Roberto (2022): "Aggregate Confusion: The Divergence of ESG Ratings", in: *Review of Finance*, 26/6, 1315–1344, https://doi.org/10.1093/rof/rfac033.

Bermejo Carbonell, Jorge; Werner, Richard (2018): "Does Foreign Direct Investment Generate Economic Growth? A New Empirical Approach Applied to Spain", in: *Economic Geography*, 94/4, 425–456, https://doi.org/10.1080/00130095.2017.1393312.

Bevilacqua, Marco et al. (2024): "Global Energy Perspective 2023: Energy Value Pools Outlook", https://www.mckinsey.com/industries/oil-and-gas/our-insights/global-energy-perspective-2023-energy-value-pools-outlook.

Beyond Bretton Woods (2024): "Ten Deep Financial System Recommendations", https://www.beyondbrettonwoods.org/recommendations.

Böick, Marcus; Lorke, Christoph (2019): "Aufschwung, Abbau, Anpassung? Eine kleine Geschichte des, Aufbau Ost'", in: *APuZ*, 46, 32–40, https://www.bpb.de/shop/zeitschriften/apuz/300059/aufschwung-abbau-anpassung/.

Bongaerts, Dion; Cremers, K.J. Martijn; Goethmann, William (2009): Multiple Ratings and Credit Spreads, Yale ICF Working Paper No. 08–27, https://efa2009.efa-meetings.org/www.efa2009.org/papers/SSRN-id1307782.pdf.

Borio, Claudio; Furfine, Craig; Lowe, Philip (2001): "Procyclicality of the Financial System and Financial Stability: Issues and Policy Options", in: Bank for International Settlements (Ed.): *Marrying the Macro- and Micro-Prudential Dimensions of Financial Stability*, 1–57, https://www.bis.org/publ/bppdf/bispap01a.pdf.

Bradie, Michael; Harms, William (2020): Evolutionary Epistemology, in: *Stanford Encyclopedia of Philosophy,* https://plato.stanford.edu/entries/epistemology-evolutionary/.

Braveboy-Wagner, Jacqueline Anne (2024): "Introduction: The Global South and the Multipolar Moment", in: Braveboy-Wagner, Jacqueline Anne (Eds.): *Diplomatic Strategies of Rising Nations in the Global South*, Cham: Palgrave Macmillan, https://doi.org/10.1007/978-3-031-52629-9_1.

Bristow, Jamie et al. (2024): "The System within: Addressing the Inner Dimensions of Sustainability and Systems Transformation", EARTH4ALL: Deep Dive Paper 17, https://www.clubofrome.org/wp-content/uploads/2024/05/Earth4All_Deep_Dive_Jamie_Bristow.pdf.

Brunnenmeier, Markus K.; Reis, Ricardo (2023): *Crash Course on Crisis: Macroeconomic Concepts for Run-Ups, Collapses, and Recoveries*, Princeton: Princeton University Press.

Brunnhuber, Stefan (2020): *The Tao of Finance: The Future Wealth of Nations*, München: Oekom-Verlag.

Brunnhuber, Stefan (2021): *Financing Our Future: Unveiling a Parallel Digital Currency System to Fund the SDGs and the Common Good*, London: Palgrave Macmillan.

Brunnhuber, Stefan (2023): *Financing our Anthropocene: How Wall Street, Main Street and Central Banks Can Manage, Fund and Hedge Our Global Commons*, Berlin, Heidelberg: Springer.

Brunnhuber, Stefan (2024): *The Third Culture: The Impact of AI on Knowledge, Society and Consciousness in the 21st Century*, Berlin, Heidelberg: Springer.

Brunnhuber, Stefan; Bernhard, Lietaer (2005): "Economics as an Evolutionary System - Psychological Development and Economic Behaviour", in: *Evolutionary and Institutional Economics Review* 2, 113–139. https://doi.org/10.14441/eier.2.113

Brunnhuber, Stefan; Jacobs, Garry (2020): "Innovative Financial Engineering to Fund the SDGs: A WAAS Initiative", in: *Cadmus*, 4/2, 141–148, https://www.cadmusjournal.org/node/783.

Buchanan, Mark (2013): *Forecast – What Physics, Meteorology, and the Natural Sciences Can Teach Us About Economics*, London: Bloomsbury.

Buchner, Barbara et al. (2023): *Global Landscape of Climate Finance 2023*, San Francisco: Climate Policy Initiative.

Callen, Tim (2024): "Purchasing Power Parity: Weights Matter", in: *IMF Website*, https://www.imf.org/en/Publications/fandd/issues/Series/Back-to-Basics/Purchasing-Power-Parity-PPP.

Carbon Majors (2024): "The Carbon Majors Databas: Launch Report", https://carbon-majors.org/briefing/The-Carbon-Majors-Database-26913.

Carson, Rachel (1962): *Silent Spring*, Boston: Mifflin Harcourt.

CDP (2023): "Scoping Out: Tracking Nature Across the Supply Chain", https://cdn.cdp.net/cdp-production/cms/reports/documents/000/006/918/original/CDP-Supply-Chain-Report-2022.pdf?1678870769.

Center for Global Development (2023): "Strengthening Multilateral Development Banks: The Triple Agenda", Report of the independent experts group, https://www.cgdev.org/publication/strengthening-multilateral-development-banks-triple-agenda.

Centre for Thriving Places (2024): "The Thriving Places Index", https://www.thrivingplacesindex.org.

Chakrabasty, Dipesh (2021): *The Climate of History in a Planetary Age*, Chicago: University of Chicago Press.

Climate Analytics (2023). "Carbon Majors' Trillion Dollar Damages", https://climate-analytics.org/publications/carbon-majors-trillion-dollar-damages.

Climate Policy Initiative (2023): "Global Landscape of Climate Finance 2023", https://www.climatepolicyinitiative.org/wp-content/uploads/2023/11/Executive-Summary-1-Global-Landscape-of-Climate-Finance-2023.pdf.

Club of Rome (2024): "Rethinking Finance Impact Hub", https://www.clubofrome.org/impact-hubs/rethinking-finance/.

Cobb, Charles W.; Douglas. Paul H. (1928): "A Theory of Production", in: *The American Economic Review*, 18/1, 139–165, https://www.jstor.org/stable/1811556.

Cobham, Alex; Janský, Petr (2018): "Global Distribution of Revenue Loss from Corporate Tax Avoidance: Re-Estimation and Country Results", in: *Journal of International Development*, 30/2, 206–232, https://doi.org/10.1002/jid.3348.

Cort, Todd; Esty, Daniel (2020). "ESG Standards: Looming Challenges and Pathways Forward", in: *Organization & Environment*, 33/4, 491–510, https://doi.org/10.1177/1086026620945342.

Council on Foreign Relations (2024): "Central Bank Currency Swaps Tracker", https://www.cfr.org/article/central-bank-currency-swaps-tracker.

Damgaard, Jannick; Elkjaer, Thomas; Johannesen, Niels (2019). "The Rise of Phantom Investments", in: *Finance & Development*, 56/3, 11–13, https://www.imf.org/external/pubs/ft/fandd/2019/09/ the-rise-of-phantom-FDI-in-tax-havens-damgaard.htm.

Damrich, Sebastian; Kealey, Terence; Ricketts, Martin (2022): "Crowding In And Crowding Out within A Contribution Good Model of Research", in *Research Policy*, 51/1, 104400, https://www.sciencedirect.com/science/article/pii/S0048733321001967.

Dasgupta, Partha (2021): *The Economics of Biodiversity: The Dasgupta Review*, London: HM Treasury, https://assets.publishing.service.gov.uk/media/602e92b2e90e07660f807b47/The_Economics_of_Biodiversity_The_Dasgupta_Review_Full_Report.pdf.

De Soto, Hernando (2015): "Les Pauvres Contre Piketty", in: *Le Point 2015-04-16*, https://www.lepoint.fr/editos-du-point/sebastien-le-fol/les-pauvres-contre-piketty-16-04-2015-1922011_1913.php#11.

De Soto, Hernando; Cheneval, Francis (2006): *Swiss Human Rights Book Volume 1: Realizing Property Rights*, Zürich: Rüffer & Rub.

Desan, Christine A. (2022): "The Key to Value (2.0): The Debate Over Commensurability in Neoclassical and Credit Approaches to Money", in: Feichtner, I. and Gordon, G. (Eds.): *Constitutions of Value: Law, Governance and Political Ecology*, London: Routledge. pp. 134–150.

Deutz, Andrew et al. (2020): *Financing Nature: Closing the Global Biodiversity Financing Gap,* Chicago: Paulson Institute, https://www.paulsoninstitute.org/conservation/financing-nature-report/.

Dooley, Michael; Folkert-Landau, David; Garber, Peter (2004): "The Revived Bretton Woods System", in: *International Journal of Finance & Economics*, 9/4, 307–313, https://doi.org/10.1002/ijfe.250.

Dörner, Dietrich (1996): *The Logic of Failure: Recognizing And Avoiding Error In Complex Situations*, New York: Metropolitan Books.

Dotzauer, Marius (2023): *The Popular Legitimacy of Investor State: Contestation, Crisis, and Reform*, London: Routledge.

Douglas, Peter H. (1976): "The Cobb-Douglas Production Function Once Again: Its History, Its Testing, and Some New Empirical Values", in: *Journal of Political Economy*, 84/5, 903–916, https://doi.org/10.1086/260489.

Dutta, Sahil Jai (2018): "Financialisation: A Primer, Changefinance.org", https://www.tni.org/en/publication/financialisation-a-primer.

EFRAG (2024): "The First Set of ESRS", https://www.efrag.org/lab6.

Egmond, Klaas van; Vries, Bert de (2024): "Reforming the Eurozone Financial System: A System-Dynamics Approach", in: International Review of Financial Analysis, 93, 103192, https://doi.org/10.1016/j.irfa.2024.103192.

Eichengreen, Barry (2019): *Globalizing Capital: A History of the International Monetary System*, 3rd Edition, Princeton: Princeton University Press.

Ellul, Andrew (2014): "Mark-to-Market Accounting and Systemic Risk: Evidence from the Insurance Industry", in: *Economic Policy*, 29/78, 297–341, https://doi.org/10.1111/1468-0327.12030.

Enenkel, Kathrin; Rösel, Felix (2022): "German Reunification: Lessons from the German Approach to Closing Regional Economic Divides", in: *Navigating Economic Change Series*, https://economy2030.resolutionfoundation.org/reports/german-reunification/.

EU Block Chain Observatory and Forum (2024): "EUBOF Conclusion Report", https://blockchain-observatory.ec.europa.eu/publications/eubof-conclusion-report_en.

European Commission (2024): "Corporate Sustainability Due Diligence", https://commission.europa.eu/business-economy-euro/doing-business-eu/corporate-sustainability-due-diligence_en.

European Environment Agency (2024): "European Climate Risk Assessment", EEA Report 01/2024, European Environment Agency, https://www.eea.europa.eu/publications/european-climate-risk-assessment.

Fama, Eugene F.; MacBeth, James D. (1973): "Risk, Return, and Equilibrium: Empirical Tests", in: *Journal of Political Economy*, 81/3, 607–636, https://doi.org/10.1086/260061.

Ferguson, Niall (2008): *The Ascent of Money*, London: Penguin.

Ferri, Giovanni; Liu, Li-Gang (2003): "How Do Global Credit-Rating Agencies Rate Firms from Developing Countries?", in: *Asian Economic Papers*, 2/3, 30–56, https://doi.org/10.1162/asep.2003.2.3.30.

Finance Watch (2024): "Policy Portal", https://www.finance-watch.org/policy-portal/.

Flyvbjerg, Bent et al. (2018): "Five Things You Should Know about Cost Overrun", in: *Transportation Research, Part A*, 118, 174–190, https://doi.org/10.1016/j.tra.2018.07.013.

Flyvbjerg, Bent; Gardner, Dan (2024): *How Big Things Get Done: The Surprising Factors That Determine the Fate of Every Project, from Home Renovations to Space Exploration and Everything In Between*, New York: Currency.

Force for Good (2024): "Technology as a Force for Good Technology Driving the Transition to a Superior Future", https://www.forcegood.org/frontend/img/2024-report/pdf/2024_Technology_as_a_Force_for_Good_Report_v.1.2_09-01.pdf.

Galafassi, Norma (2023): "Worldwide and LATAM Giving: A Trip to the World of Giving Data in 2023, Ideas and Trends for the Future, https://in2action.net/en/how-giving-worked-in-the-world-in-2023-part-1-2/.

Gallagher, Kevin P.; Kozul-Wright, Richard (2022): *The Case for A New Bretton Woods*, New York: Wiley.

Georgieva, Kristalina (2020): "Opening Address, 2020 Spring Meeting", in: *International Monetary Funds Website*, https://www.imf.org/en/News/Articles/2020/04/15/tr041520-transcript-of-imf-md-kristalina-georgieva-opening-press-conference-2020-spring-meetings.

German Marshall Plan (2024): "The Spirit of the Marshall Plan", https://www.gmfus.org/spirit-marshall-plan.

Goodhart, Charles (1975): "Problem of Monetary Management: The U.K. Experience", in: *Papers in Monetary Economics*, 1/1, 1–20.

Greengard, Samuel (2021): *The Internet of Things*, Boston, Massachusetts, MIT Press.

Gütschow, Johannes et al. (2021): "Country-Resolved Combined Emission and Socio-Economic Pathways Based on the Representative Concentration Pathway (RCP) and Shared Socio-Economic Pathway (SSP) Scenarios", in: *Earth System Science Data*, 13/3, 1005–1040, https://doi.org/10.5194/essd-13-1005-2021.

Habbel, Valerie et al. (2021), *Evaluating Blended Finance Instruments and Mechanisms: Approaches and Methods*, OECD Development Co-operation Working Paper No. 101, Paris: Organisation for Economic Co-operation and Development.

Harari, Yuval Noah (2014): *Sapiens: A Brief History of Humankind*, New York: Random House.

Hau, Harald; Langfield, Sam; Marques-Ibanez, David (2013): "Bank Ratings: What Determines their Quality?", in: *Economic Policy*, 28/74, 289–333.

He, Jia; Hu, Wenwei; Lang, Larry H.P. (2000): "Credit Spread Curves and Credit Ratings", https://ssrn.com/abstract=224393.

Hickel, Jason (2020): "Quantifying National Responsibility for Climate Breakdown: An Equality-Based Attribution Approach for Carbon Dioxide Emissions in Excess of the Planetary Boundary", in: *Lancet Planet Health*, 4, e399–404, https://doi.org/10.1016/S2542-5196(20)30196-0.

Hickel, Jason et al. (2022): "Imperialist Appropriation in the World Wconomy: Drain from the Global South through Unequal Exchange, 1990–2015", in: *Global Environmental Change*, 73, 102467, https://doi.org/10.1016/j.gloenvcha.2022.102467.

Hiebert, Paul; Monnin, Pierre (2023): "Climate-Related Systemic Risks and Macroprudential Policy", INSPIRE Sustainable Central Banking Toolbox Paper 14, https://www.lse.ac.uk/granthaminstitute/publication/climate-related-systemic-risks-and-macroprudential-policy/.

Huber, Joseph (2024): *The Monetary Turning Point: From Bank Money to Central Bang Digital Currency (CBDC)*, London: Palgrave Macmillan.

Human Security for All (2024): "HS4A – Human Security for ALL", https://humansecurity.world.

Hung, Mingyi et al. (2022): "Market Power and Credit Rating Standards: Global Evidence", in: *Journal of Accounting and Economics*, 73/2–3, 101474, https://doi.org/10.1016/j.jacceco.2021.101474.

IMF Datamapper (2023): "General Government Gross Debt: Percent of GDP", https://www.imf.org/external/datamapper/GGXWDG_NGDP@WEO/OEMDC/ADVEC/WEOWORLD/CHN.

IMF (2023a): "Global Financial Stability Report: Financial and Climate Policies for a High-Interest-Rate Era", International Monetary Fund 2023, https://www.imf.org/en/Publications/GFSR/Issues/2023/10/10/global-financial-stability-report-october-2023.

Inner Development Goals (2024): "Inner Development Goals: Transformational Skills for Sustainable Development", https://innerdevelopmentgoals.org.

Institut Rosseau (2024): "Road to Net Zero: Bridging the Green Investment Gap", https://institut-rousseau.fr/road-2-net-zero-en/.

International Institute for Sustainable Development (2024): "Annual SDG Financing Gaps Measured in Trillions: FSDR 2024", https://sdg.iisd.org/news/annual-sdg-financing-gaps-measured-in-trillions-fsdr-2024/#:~:text="Achieving%20the%20economic%20transitions%20needed,and%20USD%204%20trillion%20annually.

IPCC (2023): "Summary for Policymakers", in: *Climate Change 2023: Synthesis Report. Contribution of Working Groups I, II and III to the Sixth Assessment Report of the Intergovernmental Panel on Climate Change,* Geneva: IPCC, https://www.ipcc.ch/report/ar6/syr/downloads/report/IPCC_AR6_SYR_SPM.pdf.

Issa, R; Robin van Daalen, K; Faddoul, A; Collias, L; James, R; Chaudhry, UAR et al. (2023) Human migration on a heating planet: A scoping review. PLOS Clim 2(5): e0000214. https://doi.org/10.1371/journal.pclm.0000214

Jackson, Andrew (2013): *Sovereign Money: Paving the Way to a Sustainable Recovery*, London: Positive Money.

Jackson, Andrew; Dyson, Ben (2012): *Modernising Money: Why Our Montary System is Broken and How it Can be Fixed*, London: Positive Money.

Jacobs, Garry; Šlaus, Ivo (2012): "The Power of Money", in: *Cadmus*, 1/5, 68–73. https://cadmusjournal.org/files/journalpdf/Vol4Issue4/Vol4_Issue4.pdf

Jess, Tom; Blom, Peter; Dixson-Declève, Sandrine (2023): "From Financing Change to Changing Finance", in: *The Club of Rome* November 2023, https://www.clubofrome.org/wp-content/uploads/2023/10/Changing_Finance_2023-3.pdf.

Johnson, Emma (2017): "Health and Social Care Spending Cuts Linked to 120,000 Excess Deaths in England", in: *BMJ*, https://www.sciencedaily.com/releases/2017/11/171115195300.htm.

Johnson, Lise; Sachs, Lisa; Lobel, Nathan (2019): "Aligning International Investment Agreements with the Sustainable Development Goals", in: *Columbia Journal of Transnational Law*, 58/1, 58–120, https://ccsi.columbia.edu/sites/default/files/content/docs/publications/Briefing-Aligning-International-Investment-Agreements-with-the-Sustainable-Development-Goals.pdf.

Keen, Steven; Ayres, Robert U.; Standish, Russell (2019): "A Note on the Role of Energy in Production", in: *Ecological Economics*, 157, 40–46, https://doi.org/10.1016/j.ecolecon.2018.11.002.

Keen, Steven (forthcoming): *Rebuilding Economics from the Top Down*, London: Pallas Athene.

Khanna, Rohit; Healy, Claire (2023): "The World Needs a Bank for Global Public Goods and the World Bank Should Be Reformed to Play that Role", *Consultation, Indian Council for Research*, https://icrier.org.

Kindleberger, Charles P. (1987): "Capital Flight – A Historical Perspective", in: Lessard, Donald R., Williamson, John (Eds.): *Capital Flight: The Problem and Policy Responses*, Washington: Institute for International Economics.

Kisling, Lisa A., Das, Joe M. (2023): *Prevention Strategies*. Treasure Island (FL): StatPearls Publishing, https://www.ncbi.nlm.nih.gov/books/NBK537222/.

Kissinger, Henry (2014): *World Order*, New York: Pinguin Press.

Kubiszewski, Ida; Costanza, Robert; Franco, Carol; Lawn, Philip; Talberth, John; Jackson, Tim; Aylmer, Camille (September 2013): "Beyond GDP: Measuring and Achieving Global Genuine Progress", in: *Ecological Economics*, 93, 57–68. https://doi.org/10.1016/j.ecolecon.2013.04.019.

Kuhn, Thomas (1962): *The Structure of Scientific Revolutions*, Chicago: University of Chicago Press.

Kumhof, Michael; Noone, Clare (2021): "Central Bank Digital Currencies – Design Principles for Financial Stability", in: *Economic Analysis and Policy*, 71/C, 553–572, https://doi.org/10.1016/j.eap.2021.06.012.

Kümmel, Reiner (2013): "Why Energy's Economic Weight is Much Larger than Its Cost Share", in: *Environmental Innovation and Societal Transitions* 9/December 2013, 33–37, https://doi.org/10.1016/j.eist.2013.09.003.

Kyla, Tienhaara et al. (2022): "Investor-State Disputes Threaten the Global Green Energy Transition", in: *Science*, 376, 701–3, https://doi.org/10.1126/science.abo4637.

Larsen, Lotta Björkland (2018): *A Fair Share of Tax: A Fiscal Anthropology of Contemporary Sweden*, London: Palgrave Macmillan.

Lazard (2022): "How to Make Sovereign Debt Restructuring More Effective: How Warring Parties to a Better Standard of 'Comparability'", *Policy Brief*, https://www.lazard.com/media/c5bb0n11/lazard-policy-brief-on-comparability-of-treatment-may-2022.pdf.

Leaven, Luc; Valencia, Fabián (2012): "Systemic Banking Crises Database: An Update", IMF Working Paper 12/163, https://www.imf.org/external/pubs/ft/wp/2012/wp12163.pdf.

Li, Yuefen (2021): "It Is High Time to Implement A Major Reform of Credit-Rating Agencies", in: *International Banker*, June 16th 2021, https://internationalbanker.com/finance/it-is-high-time-to-implement-a-major-reform-of-credit-rating-agencies/.

Lietaer 2001, Bernhard (2001): *The Future of Money: Beyond Greed and Scarcity*, New York: Random House.

Lo, Andrew W. (2017): *Adaptive Markets: Financial Evolution at the Speed of Thought*, Princeton: Princeton University Press.

Lomborg, Bjørn (2023): *Best Things First: The 12 Most Efficient Solutions for the World's Poorest and our Global SDG Promises*, Copenhagen: Copenhagen Consensus Center.

Lucas, Robert. (1990): "Why Doesn't Capital Flow from Rich to Poor Countries?", American Economic Review 80(2), 92–96.

Lucas, Robert E. (1976): "Econometric Policy Evaluation: A Critique", in: *Carnegie-Rochester Conference Series on Public Policy*, 1, 19–46, https://doi.org/10.1016/S0167-2231(76)80003-6.

MacAskill, William (2017): "Effective Altruism: Introduction", in: *Essays in Philosophy*, 18/1, 1–5, https://dx.doi.org/10.7710/1526-0569.1580.

Mainzer, Klaus (1997): *Thinking in Complexity: The Complexity Dynamics of Matter, Mind, and Mankind*, Berlin, Heidelberg: Springer.

Malewska, Alicja (2021): "Failed Attempt to Break Up the Oligopoly in Sovereign Credit Rating Market after Financial Crises", in: *Contemporary Economics*, 15/2, 152–163, https://ssrn.com/abstract=3850584.

Mandelbrot, Benoît (1977): *Fractals: Form, Chance, and Dimension*, San Francisco: W. H. Freeman.

Markowitz, Harry M. (1959): *Portfolio Selection: Efficient Diversification of Investments*, New Haven: Yale University Press.

Marois, Thomas; Stewart, Jacob; Marodon, Régis (2024): *From Multi- to National-and Back Again: Realizing the SDG Potential of Public Development Banks*, Éditions AFD: Research Papers, https://www.cairn-int.info/revue-afd-research-papers-2023-267-page-1.htm.

Masala, Carlo (2022): *Weltunordnung: Die globalen Krisen und die Illusionen des Westens*, München: C.H. Beck.

Mazzucato, Mariana (2021): *Mission Economy: A Moonshot Guide to Changing Capitalism*, New York: Harper Business.

McDonald, Matt (2018): "Climate Change and Security: Towards Ecological Security?", in: *International Theory*, 10/2, 153–180, https://doi.org/10.1017/S1752971918000039.

Meadows, Donella et al. (1972): *The Limits to Growth*, Falls Church: Potomac Associates.

Meadows, Donella H. (2008): *Thinking in Systems: A Primer*, Sustainability Institute, Vermont: Chelsea Green Publishing Whit River Junction.

Megliani, Mauro (2021): "Single-Limb Collective Action Clauses and the European Stability Mechanism Reform", in: *European Business Law Review*, 32/1, 77–92, https://doi.org/10.54648/eulr2021004.

Meyer, Eva; Welpe, Isabell M.; Sander, Philipp G. (2022): *Decentralized Finance—A Systematic Literature Review and Research Directions*, ECIS 2022 Research Papers 25 https://aisel.aisnet.org/ecis2022_rp/25.

Modigliani, Franco (1986): "Life Cycle, Individual Thrift, and the Wealth of Nations", in: *New Series*, 234/4777, 704–712, https://www.jstor.org/stable/1697934.

Münkler, Herfried (2023): *Welt in Aufruhr: Die Ordnung der Mächte im 21*, Jahrhundert: Rowohlt.

Nash, John Forbes (1950): *Non-cooperative games, Dissertation*, Princeton: Princeton University 1950.

Neuwirth, Robert (2012): *Stealth of Nations: The Global Rise of the Informal Economy*, New York: Knopf Doubleday Publishing Group.

Nicita, Alessandro; Olarreaga, Marcelo; Silva, Peri (2018): "Cooperation in WTO's Tariff Waters?", in: *Journal of Political Economy*, 126/3, https://doi.org/10.1086/697085. pp. 1302–1338

OECD (2020): "A Comprehensive Overview of Global Biodiversity Finance, OECD", https://www.oecd.org/environment/resources/biodiversity/report-a-comprehensive-overview-of-global-biodiversity-finance.pdf.

Ormerod, Paul (2005): *Why Most Things Fail: Evolution, Extinction and Economics*, London: Faber and Faber Limited.

Our World in Data (2023): "People Living in Democracies and Non-Democracies", https://ourworldindata.org/grapher/people-living-in-democracies-nondemocracies-womsuffr-bmr?country=OWID_EUR~OWID_OCE~OWID_AFR~OWID_NAM~OWID_WRL~OWID_ASI~OWID_SAM.

Paduano, Stephen (2024): "A State of Play on SDRs: What To Make of 2023, What to Watch in 2024", FDL Short Notes, FDL Finance for Development Lab, https://findevlab.org/wp-content/uploads/2024/01/FDL_ShortNote_SDR_State_of_Play_Paduano_Jan24.pdf.

Peng, Sheng-Lung; Pal, Souvik; Huang, Lianfen (2020): *Principles of Internet of Things (IoT) Ecosystem: Insight Paradigm,* Switzerland: Springer, https://doi.org/10.1007/978-3-030-33596-0.

People-Centered Internet (2023): "People Centered Internet", https://peoplecentered.net.

Perks, Michael et al. (2021): "Evolution of Bilateral Swap Lines", IMF Working Paper, IMF, https://www.imf.org/-/media/Files/Publications/WP/2021/English/wpiea2021210-print-pdf.ashx.

Persaud, Avinash (2023): "Unblocking the Green Transformation in Developing Countries with a Partial Foreign Exchange Guarantee, Climate Policy Initiative", https://www.climatepolicyinitiative.org/wp-content/uploads/2023/06/An-FX-Guarantee-Mechanism-for-the-Green-Transformation-in-Developing-Countries.pdf.

Persaud, Avinash (2024): "34th Dr. Eric Williams Memorial Lecture of Avinash Persaud", in: *Central Bank of Trinidad and Tobago,* https://www.central-bank.org.tt/news-centre/latest-news/professor-avinash-persaud-discusses-how-break-climate-finance-deadlock.

Piketty, Thomas; Saez, Emmanuel; Zucman, Gabriel (2023): "Rethinking Capital and Wealth Taxation", *Oxford Review of Economic Policy*, 39, 575–591, https://doi.org/10.1093/oxrep/grad026.

Pollman, Elizabeth (2024): "The Making and Meaning of ESG", University of Penn, Institute for Law & Econ Research Paper No. 22–23, https://papers.ssrn.com/sol3/papers.cfm?abstract_id=4219857.

Pozsar, Zoltan and Adrian, Tobias and Ashcraft, Adam B. and Boesky, Hayley (2013): "Shadow Banking", in *Economic Policy Review*, 19(2), https://ssrn.com/abstract=2378449.

Prime Minister of Barbados (2023): "Bridgetown 2.0 Initiative", https://pmo.gov.bb/bridgetown2-0-2pager-3/.

Reinhart, Carmen M.; Reinhart, Vincent; Trebesch, Christoph (2016): "Global Cycles: CapitalFlows,Commodities,andSovereignDefaults,1815-2015."*AmericanEconomic Review*,106/5, 574–80, https://www.jstor.org/stable/43861085.

Richardson, Katherine et al. (2023): "Earth beyond Six of Nine Planetary Boundaries", in: *Science Advances*, 9, eadh2458, https://www.science.org/doi/10.1126/sciadv.adh2458.

Röckström, Johan et al. (2024): "The Planetary Commons: A New Paradigm for Safeguarding Earth-Regulating Systems in the Anthropocene", in: *Environmental Sciences*, 121/5, e2301531121, https://doi.org/10.1073/pnas.2301531121.

Rockström, Johan et al. (2024): "The Planetary Commons: A New Paradigm for Safeguarding Earth-Regulating Systems in the Anthropocene", in: *PNAS*, 121/5, e2301 531121, https://doi.org/10.1073/pnas.2301531121.

Saez, Emmanuel; Zucman, Gabriel (2019): "Progressive Wealth Taxation", in: BPEA. Washington, DC: Inst., ISSN 0007-2303, ZDB-ID 187008-7, 2019, 437–511.

Sattari, Reza et al. (2022): "The Ripple Effects of Funding on Researchers and Output", in: *Science Advances*, 8, eabb7348, https://doi.org/10.1126/sciadv.abb7348.

Schmucker, Claudia; Mildner, Stormy-Annika (2023): *Reforming the WTO Through Inclusive and Development-friendly Approaches: How to Make Plurilateral Initiatives Work for All*, Berling: Forschungsinstitut der Deutschen Gesellschaft für Auswärtige Politik e.V., https://www.ssoar.info/ssoar/handle/document/89986.

Schroeder, Frank (2006): "Innovative Sources of Finance after the Paris Conference: The Concept Is Gaining Currency but Major Challenges Remain", Friedrich-Ebert-Stiftung Briefing Paper, https:// library.fes.de/pdf-files/iez/global/50423.pdf.

Schularick, Moritz (2022): *The New Economics of Debt and Financial Fragility*, Chicago: University of Chicago Press, https://doi.org/10.7208/chicago/9780226816944.

Seery, Emma (2020): "50 Years of Broken Promises", Oxfam International, https://oxfamilibrary.openrepository.com/bitstream/handle/10546/621080/bn-50-years-broken-promises-aid-231020-en.pdf.

Semieniuk, Gregor et al. (2022): "Stranded Fossil-Fuel Assets Translate to Major Losses for Investors in Advanced Economies", in: *Nature Climate Change*, 12, 532–538, https://doi.org/10.1038/s41558-022-01356-y.

Setser, Brad W.; Paduano, Stephen (2022): "How an SDR Denominated Bond Could Work", Council on Foreign Relations, https://www.cfr.org/blog/how-sdr-denominated-bond-could-work#:~:text=The%20World%20Bank%20can%20issue,usable%20currencies%20through%20the%20IMF.

Shaxson, Nicholas (2018): *The Finance Curse: How Global Finance Is Making Us All Poorer*, London: Bodley Head.

Shearer, Jana (2023) "Market-to-Market: Delivering the Financial Crisis to Your Front Door", in: *Ohio Northern University Law Review*, 36/1, https://digitalcommons.onu.edu/onu_law_review/vol36/iss1/13/.

Shiller, Robert J. (2019): *Narrative Economics: How Stories Go Viral and Drive Major Economic Events*, New Jersey: Princeton University Press.

Singhania, Monica; Saini, Neha (2021): "Institutional Framework of ESG Disclosures: ComparativeAnalysis ofDevelopedandDevelopingCountries", in:*Journal ofSustainable Finance & Investment*, 13/1, 516–559, https://doi.org/10.1080/20430795.2021.1964810.

Singhania, Monica; Saini, Neha (2022). "Quantification of ESG Regulations: A Cross-Country Benchmarking Analysis", in: *Vision*, 26/2, 163–171. https://doi.org/10.1177/09722629211054173.

Sinn, Hans-Werner (2009): *Kasino-Kapitalismus: Wie es zur Finanzkrise kam, und was jetzt zu tun ist*, Berlin: Econ Verlag.

Sinn, Hans-Werner (2012): *The Green Paradox. A Supply-Side Approach to Global Warming*, Cambridge, Massachusetts: MIT Press.

Šlaus, Ivo (2020): *Transforming Our World: Necessary, Urgent, and Still Possible*, Cambridge: Cambridge Scholars Publishing.

Solow, Robert (1957): "Technical Change and the Aggregate Production Function", in: *Review of Economics and Statistics*, 39, 312–320. https://doi.org/10.2307/1926047

Songwe, Vera; Stern, Nicholas; Bhattacharya (2022): "Finance for Climate Action: Scaling up Investment for Climate and Development", Report of the Independent High-Level Expert Group on Climate Finance, Grantham Institute, https://www.lse.ac.uk/granthaminstitute/wp-content/uploads/2022/11/IHLEG-Finance-for-Climate-Action-1.pdf.

Soros, George (2009): *The Crash of 2008 and What it Means: The New Paradigm for Financial Markets*, New York: Public Affairs.

Soto, Heranando de (2001): *The Mystery Of Capital: Why Capitalism Triumphs in the West and Fails Everywhere Else*, New York: Basic Books.

Start Up Ranking (2024): "Start Up Ranking 2024", https://www.startupranking.com/countries.

Statistics.com (2024): Website: Home, https://www.statistics.com.

Stavins, Robert N. (2022): "The Relative Merits of Carbon Pricing Instruments: Taxes Versus Trading", in: *Review of Environmental Economics and Policy*, 16/1, 62–82, https://doi.org/10.1086/717773.

Strathern, Marilyn (1997): "'Improving Ratings': Audit in the British University System", in: *European Review*, 5/3, 305–321, https://doi.org/10.1002/(SICI)1234-981X(199707)5:3<305::AID-EURO184>3.0.CO;2-4.

Strom, Stephanie (2007): "2 Young Hedge-Fund Veterans Stir Up the World of Philanthropy". *The New York Times*, https://www.nytimes.com/2007/12/20/us/20charity.html.

Sukhdev, Pavan (2012): *Corporation 2020: Transforming Business for Tomorrow's World*, Washington: Island Press.

SWIFT (2024): "Discover SWIFT", https://www.swift.com/de/node/10971.

Taleb, Nassim (2012): *Antifragile: Things That Gain from Disorder*, New York: Random House.

Tamez, Mario; Weenink, Hans; Yoshinaga, Akihiro (2024): *Central Banks and Climate Change: Key Legal Issues*, IMF Working Paper No. 24/192, Washington: International Monetary Fund.

The Global Economy (2024): "Savings, in Dollars - Country Rankings", https://www.theglobaleconomy.com/rankings/savings_dollars/.

The Guardian (2023): "$700m pledged to loss and damage fund at Cop28 covers less than 0.2% needed", in: *The Guardian*, 6 Dec 2023, https://www.theguardian.com/environment/2023/dec/06/700m-pledged-to-loss-and-damage-fund-cop28-covers-less-than-02-percent-needed.

The World Bank (2021): "From Accounts to Policy: WAVES closeout report Wealth Accounting and Valuation of Ecosystem Services (WAVES) Global Partnership: 2012–2019", https://documents1.worldbank.org/curated/en/779351636579119839/pdf/From-Accounts-to-Policy-WAVES-Closeout-Report-Wealth-Accounting-and-Valuation-of-Ecosystem-Services-Global-Partnership-2012-2019.pdf.

The World Bank (2023): "World Development Indicators", https://databank.worldbank.org/home.

The World Bank (2024a): Voting Powers, https://www.worldbank.org/en/about/leadership/votingpowers.

The World Bank (2024b): "World Bank Group Prepares Major Overhaul to Guarantee Business", https://www.worldbank.org/en/news/press-release/2024/02/27/world-bank-group-prepares-major-overhaul-to-guarantee-business.

Thelwall, Mike et al. (2023): "What is Research Funding, How does It Influence Research, and How Is It Recorded? Key Dimensions of Variation", in: *Scientometrics*, 128, 6085–6106, https://doi.org/10.1007/s11192-023-04836-w.

Tobin, James (1989): "Reviewed Work: Stabilizing an Unstable Economy. Hyman P. Minsky", in: *Journal of Economic Literature*, 27/1, 105–108, https://www.jstor.org/stable/2726964.

Transparency International (2022): "Corruptions Perceptions Index 2022", https://www.transparency.org/en/cpi/2022.

Uexkull, Nina von; Buhaug, Halvard (2021): "Security Implications of Climate Change: A Decade of Scientific Progress", in: *Journal of Peace Research*, 58/1, 3–17, https://doi.org/10.1177/00223433209842. https://journals.sagepub.com/doi/10.1177/0022343320984210.

UN Global Crisis Response Group (2023): *A World of Dept: A Growing Burden to Global Prosperity*, New York: United Nations, https://unctad.org/system/files/official-document/osgmisc_2023d4_en.pdf.

UNCTAD (2015): *Investment Policy Framework for Sustainable Development 2015*, New York: United Nations, https://unctad.org/system/files/official-document/diaepcb2015d5_en.pdf.

United Nations (2009): "World Economic Situation and Prospects 2009", United Nations, https://www.un.org/en/development/desa/policy/wesp/wesp_archive/2009wesp.pdf.

UN Environment Programme (2023): "Adaptation Gap Report 2023", https://www.unep.org/resources/adaptation-gap-report-2023.

Vasic-Lalovic, Ivana; Merling, Lara; Wu, Aileen (2023): "The Growing Debt Burdens of Global South Countries: Standing in the Way of Climate and Development Goals", Center of Economic Policy Research (CEPR), https://cepr.net/wp-content/uploads/2023/10/The-Growing-Debt-Burdens-of-Global-South-Countries_Standing-in-the-Way-of-Climate-and-Development-Goals-Lalovic-Merling-Wu.pdf

Verbaanderd, Ciska; Rooman, Ilse; Huys, Isabelle (2021): "Exploring New Uses for Existing Drugs: Innovative Mechanisms to Fund Independent Clinical Research", in: *Trials*, 22/322, 2–13. https://doi.org/10.1186/s13063-021-05273-x. 2–13.

Vollmer, Gerhard (1975): *Evolutionäre Erkenntnistheorie*, Stuttgart: Hirzel-Verlag.

Volz, Ulrich; Lo, Yuen C.; Mishra, Vaibhav (2024), *Scaling Up Green Investment in Global South, Strengthening Domestic Financial Resource Mobilisation, and Attracting Patient International Capital*, London: SOAS Centre for Sustainable Finance, https://doi.org/10.25501/SOAS.00041078.

Volz, Ulrich et al. (2020): *Debt Relief for a Green and Inclusive Recovery: A Proposal*, Berlin, London, and Boston: Heinrich-Böll-Stiftung; SOAS, University of London; and Boston University, https://www.boell.de/sites/default/files/2021-01/Endf%20DRGR%20Hauptreport%20%28klein%29.pdf.

Vulnerable Club of the 20 (2024): "About, V20 Website", https://www.v-20.org/about.

Wang, Yan; Qian, Ying (2022): "In Debt Restructuring, is a 'Haircut' Better than 'Rescheduling?' New Research Shows They are Comparable Approaches", Boston University Global Development Policy Center, https://www.bu.edu/gdp/2022/09/21/in-debt-restructuring-is-a-haircut-better-than-rescheduling-new-research-shows-they-are-comparable-approaches/.

Welzer, Harald (2011): "Mental Infrastructures: How Growth Entered the World and Our Souls", Volume 14 of the Publication Series on Ecology edited by the Heinrich Böll Foundation, https://www.boell.de/sites/default/files/endf_mental_infrastructures.pdf.

Werner, Richard A. (2014): "Can Banks Individually Create Money out of Nothing? — The Theories and the Empirical Evidence", in: *International Review of Financial Analysis* December 2014, 36, 1–19, https://doi.org/10.1016/j.irfa.2014.07.015.

White, Lawrence J. (2019): "The Credit Rating Agencies and Their Role in the Financial System", in: Brousseau, Eric; Glachant, Jean-Michel; Sgard, Jérôme (Eds.): *Oxford Handbook on Institutions, International Economic Governance, and Market Regulation*, Oxford: Oxford University Press, https://doi.org/10.1093/oxfordhb/9780190900571.013.38.

Williamson, John (1990): "What Washington Means by Policy Reform", in: Williamson, John (Ed.): *Latin American Readjustment: How Much has Happened*, Washington: Institute for International Economics, pp. 7–12.

Williamson, John (2008): "A Short History of the Washington Consensus", in Serra, Narcís; Stiglitz, Joseph E. (Eds.): *The Washington Consensus Reconsidered*, Oxford: Oxford University Press, 14–30.

Woetzel, Lola et al. (2021): "The Rise and Rise of the Global Balance Sheet: How Productively Are We Using Our Wealth?", McKinsey Global Institute, https://www.mckinsey.com/industries/financial-services/our-insights/the-rise-and-rise-of-the-global-balance-sheet-how-productively-are-we-using-our-wealth#/.

World Academy of Art and Sciences (2024): "The Tao of Finance", https://worldacademy.org/tao-of-finance/.

World Trade Organization (2023): "WTO Secretariat Budget for 2024", https://www.wto.org/english/thewto_e/secre_e/budget_e.htm.

Worldometer (2024): "GDP by Country", https://www.worldometers.info/gdp/gdp-by-country/.

Wullweber, Joscha (2020): "Embedded Finance: The Shadow Banking System, Sovereign Power, and A New State-Market Hybridity", in: *Journal of Cultural Economy*, 13/5, 592–609, https://doi.org/10.1080/17530350.2020.1741015.

Zhou, Xiaochuan (2009): "Reform the International Monetary System", *BIS Review, Bank of Internatinal Settlements*, https://www.bis.org/review/r090402c.pdf.

Zucker-Marques, Marina et al. (2023): "Debt Relief by Multilateral Lenders: Why, How and How Much?", Debt Relief for a Green & Inclusive Recover, https://www.boell.de/sites/default/files/2023-09/drgr-report-2023-digitalversion-final.pdf.

Index

Note: **Bold** page numbers refer to tables; *italic* page numbers refer to figures and page numbers followed by "n" denote endnotes.

Kolibri 360 GmbH
Ferdinand-Jühlke-Straße 7
99095 Erfurt, Deutschland
produktsicherheit@kolibri360.de